FULLNESS OF JOY

FULLNESS OF JOY

Ambassador International
GREENVILLE, SOUTH CAROLINA & BELFAST, NORTHERN IRELAND

www.ambassador-international.com

FULLNESS OF JOY
One Hundred Devotions to Bring You Into God's Presence
©2024 by Interim HealthCare of Upstate 2024
All rights reserved

ISBN: 978-1-64960-701-0, hardcover
ISBN: 978-1-64960-704-1, paperback
eISBN: 978-1-64960-718-8

Cover Design by Karen Slayne
Interior Typesetting by Dentelle Design
Edited by Katie Cruice Smith

Unless otherwise noted Scripture quoted are from The New International Version NIV. Copyright 1973, 1978, 1984, 2011 by Biblica, Inc. Used by permission of Zondervan. All rights reserved.

Scripture marked KJV taken from the King James Version of the Bible. Public Domain.

Scripture marked NKJV taken from The New King James Version. Copyright 1982 by Thomas Nelson. Used by permission. All rights reserved.

Scripture marked NLT taken from The New Living Translation, copyright 1996, 2004, 2015 by Tyndale House Foundation. Used by permission of Tyndale House Publishers, Carol Stream, Illinois 60188. All rights reserved.

Ambassador International titles may be purchased in bulk for education, business, fundraising, or sales promotional use. For information, please email sales@emeraldhouse.com.

AMBASSADOR INTERNATIONAL
Emerald House
411 University Ridge, Suite B14
Greenville, SC 29601
United States
www.ambassador-international.com

AMBASSADOR BOOKS
The Mount
2 Woodstock Link
Belfast, BT6 8DD
Northern Ireland, United Kingdom
www.ambassadormedia.co.uk

The colophon is a trademark of Ambassador, a Christian publishing company.

"You will show me the path of life; In Your presence is fullness of joy; At Your right hand are pleasures forevermore."

—Psalm 16:11 (NKJV)

Table of Contents

Foreword

The day Ray and I met Walt and Libby Handford was a watershed moment of my life. Over thirty-five years after that first meeting, Libby's wisdom, compassion, and quest for understanding still influence me. She lives every second of every day in step with Jesus Christ—His teachings, prayers, and direction. She naturally and beautifully shares her wisdom with everyone she meets, relating to all.

After that first pivotal meeting, Libby quickly and quietly became a bedrock of the Interim HealthCare culture. Her weekly devotional spoke to our people as we experienced extreme business growth, personal tragedy, reorganization, network and software changes, leadership changes, and the pandemic in 2020 and 2021. She applies God's Holy Word to any individual or professional situation. She is a blessing beyond words.

Libby is uniquely gifted to apply and share the Scripture. She has read the Bible in its entirety at least once nearly every year for over eighty years! I pray her wisdom inspires you, as it has so inspired me. Please join me in walking through a piece of the history of the Interim HealthCare of the Upstate as reflected in these beautiful devotionals.

—CHARYL SCHROEDER
Former Owner and CEO of Interim HealthCare of the Upstate

Author's Note

Walt Handford served as a pastor of Southside Baptist Church (now Fellowship Greenville) for thirty-one years. He had given his life to bringing people to Jesus and shepherding them into an intimate relationship with Him. When he retired at the age of seventy-three, he felt absolutely bereft, like he had lost his wonderful purpose in life. But three months later, after the commissioning service for the new pastor, Dr. Charlie Boyd, friends invited us to lunch with Ray and Charyl Schroeder. We knew them casually but not well.

Walt asked Ray what he did for a living. When Ray told him about the scope of Interim HealthCare of the Upstate, Walt said, "Oh, what a wonderful opportunity to reach people for Jesus!"

That week, Ray phoned. "Walt, you've set my heart on fire. Will you and Libby come and help us reach people for Jesus?"

And so for the next twelve years, until shortly before Walt's death, we had the great joy of ministering to patients and employees. What a delight it was to bring comfort and healing to so many. In 2006, I began to write a weekly devotional to encourage our employees. As of this writing, I have written the one thousandth one. I hope you will be encouraged and strengthened in your walk with the Lord Jesus by this "sampler" chosen by Interim.

—ELIZABETH HANDFORD

1
The Cost of Caring

When I was a little girl and heard the tinkling bell of the ice cream bicycle-cart on a lazy summer day on Ninth Street in Dallas, I would ask Daddy for a nickel.

Sometimes, he would fake a sigh as he dug into his pocket for a nickel and said, "Like Sir Francis Bacon said, 'He who has children gives hostages to fortune.'" Then he'd smile as I ran out the door.

I had no idea what the saying meant. I thought maybe he was glad God had given him six little girls for whom to buy ice cream cones. It was not until we had our own dear little mob of seven that I understood. There is a cost to loving someone. There is a price to pay when you have a great dream to fulfill. Once you have given your heart to something great, you cannot just back away from it when things get hard.

Walt and I learned this when he was a pastor. Because we cared about the people God had put into our lives, we could not make decisions without keeping their welfare in mind. When we care about the people with whom we work and those we serve, we cannot just shrug off the burden when things get difficult.

A mother cannot say, "I'm too tired to be a mother today." She has to put her children's needs first. A friend does not say, "I'm giving up on this friendship. It costs too much." Friendship is an obligation not lightly set aside. But here is the good news from the Holy God Who created you and gave you those blessings sometimes disguised as burdens. He tells us in Psalm 103:13-14, "The LORD is like a father to his children, tender and compassionate to those who fear him. For he knows how weak we are; he remembers we are only dust." God knows the relentless burdens you carry. He has promised to help you carry them. And He is faithful!

2
How to Get Smart

It's sort of embarrassing to be eighty-two years old and have your very own child say, "Mother, there's a better way to do that. Let me show you."

I can respond in one of two ways. I can say, "I am your mother, and I ought to know what's best." Or I can say, "Great! Show me."

This brings to mind a Scripture Walt and I read the other day. "Intelligent people are always ready to learn," says Proverbs 18:15. " Their ears are open for knowledge."

When I was a senior in college, making out my class schedule for the year, I found I'd already met all the requirements for graduation and still had four hours to fill. I decided I'd take the home economics sewing class. I'd been sewing ever since I was a freshman in high school, but I thought maybe I'd learn some shortcuts so I could do it faster.

Instead, when I got to class, I discovered there were some important but basic things I'd never learned about making clothes—partly because I was always trying to find shortcuts! I struggled with this because I felt very competent. It wasn't until I admitted to myself that I wasn't the expert I'd always considered myself to be and submitted my heart and mind to the professor that I could learn how to sew! The things I learned then have proved to be valuable for me over the years, as I used those principles in making clothes for our seven children.

I can be teachable, or I can wallow in my inadequate self-assurance. It's up to me. This choice is something I'm going to have to ask God to help me with.

3
I Can Plod

William Carey was a shoemaker in England, who came to see that the world God loves deserves to hear about Him. He left his shoemaking and went to India as a missionary. During the arduous years he served in India, he translated the Bible into two major languages—Bengali and Sanskrit—as well as several dialects, so people could have God's Word in their own languages. He was called "the father of modern missions" because of his passion to take Christ to the mission fields of the world.

Near the end of his life, this man who had accomplished so much said, "I can plod. This is my only genius. I can persevere in any definite pursuit. To this I owe everything."

There are some things about our work that are exciting and fulfilling. It's rewarding to see the results of our hard work. But sometimes, we have to do a lot of "plodding" in our work and in our homes. No matter how important our work is, some parts of it are repetitive, to be done over and over again.

But "plodding," Carey said, was the essence of his genius. He could keep doing that; he could persevere. Only eternity will reveal how many people heard the message of salvation because he was content to do the job he had set his mind to do—day after day, month after month, year after year. Today, you may have a wonderful opportunity to do something extraordinary. But it also may be that today, your job will be only to "plod," to persevere in the tasks God has assigned you to do.

As Deuteronomy 31:6 says, "So be strong and courageous! Do not be afraid and do not panic before them. For the Lord your God will personally go ahead of you. He will neither fail you nor abandon you."

4
Perilous Crossing of the Ubangi River

Walt and I once visited missionary friends in the Central African Republic (CAR), deep in the very heart of Africa. One day, the Bixbys drove us down to the Ubangi River. We planned to take a dugout canoe to cross over into the Congo. The river is very wide there, perhaps half a mile across. From CAR, the river flows westward into the Congo River and empties into the Atlantic.

We four passengers sat, single file, on the fire-charred bottom of the boat, while eight young and cheerful men stood on the rim of the boat with their paddles. Upriver, they warned us, were man-killing hippopotamuses. Down river, crocodiles lurked. It would be best, they said, to stay inside the boat.

The lead man started a chant, and the crew joined in. They headed upstream, close to the shore where the current wasn't so strong. Then they cut a diagonal toward the far shore. I naïvely thought they sang to entertain us, so I cried, "Now, Walt and I will sing for you." We began to belt out, like contestants on a talent show, the words to "You Are My Sunshine."

I think the hippopotamuses smiled when they heard Walt and me singing. Supper was about to be served! Without the chant, the crew couldn't row together. The canoe swerved and nearly floundered while they fought to bring it under control. The leader quickly began his chant again, and the crew joined in. With their synchronized rowing, the canoe steadied; and we reached the south shore safely.

The principle of synchronized teamwork is important whether you are crossing the Ubangi River, raising children, taking care of people who are ill, or reaching a community for God. We must have the same goals, the same values, the same heart, the same enthusiasm for whatever project we are working on if we are to succeed. King Solomon says in Ecclesiastes 4:9-12:

> Two people are better off than one, for they can help each other succeed. If one person falls, the other can reach out and help. But someone who falls alone is in real trouble. Likewise, two people lying close together can keep each other warm. But how can one be warm alone? A person standing alone can be attacked and defeated, but two can stand back-to-back and conquer. Three are even better, for a triple-braided cord is not easily broken.

The apostle Paul wrote something similar under the direction of the Holy Spirit in Philippians 2:2: "Then make me truly happy by agreeing wholeheartedly with each other, loving one another, and working together with one mind and purpose." May our work today be synchronized by our love and purpose!

5

While I Was Busy

First Kings 20 tells how the Israelite King Ahab wasn't doing what a good king was supposed to do: helping people do right and punishing evildoers. Instead, King Ahab was doing something else. So a prophet of God told him a parable about a soldier whose king assigned him to stand guard over a prisoner of war. But the prisoner escaped, the guard explained, while he was busy doing something else.

I thought of that story one day, when a businessman asked me about the missionary trips Walt and I took through the years. I chose some of the most intriguing and challenging trips. I described a city in central Asia so choked with humanity, the young men slept on the precarious slopes of the house roofs. There was an isolated hamlet at the end of the furthest-west paved road in America. In Africa, we slept under mosquito netting, all night hearing beating drums while crocodiles lurked in the river. We sang gospel hymns in the highlands of Southeast Asia with people whose grandfathers had been headhunters. But the purpose of our trip was to share the gospel and encourage Christians, not just to experience adventure.

The businessman listened to my stories and then said, so wistfully, "I would love to travel with my wife that way, but I only get two weeks of vacation every year."

Thinking that if he were an entrepreneur, he should be able to choose his vacation schedule, I impulsively asked, "Are you your own boss?"

"Of course, I'm my own boss," he answered.

I said no more, but I wondered: if he were his own boss, couldn't he decide his own schedule? Might he be distracted by being busy at other things?

I remembered a terrible day when lifelong friends of ours wept as they told us the wife had just been diagnosed with stage-4 cancer.

Her husband said, brokenly, through tears, "But we were going to travel together just as soon as I retired." Had they pursued less important activities, thinking they had plenty of time ahead?

That day, I realized how essential it is to be focused on the truly important responsibilities of life, rather than postponing them for later. I must choose how I spend every precious day God has given me. I ought not to focus primarily on earning a living, worrying all the time about food and clothing and shelter. Certainly, I have an obligation to take care of my family. But Jesus knows how absorbing and distracting physical needs can be. Thus He said, in Matthew 6:31-32, "'So don't worry about these things, saying, *What will we eat? What will we drink? What will we wear?*' These things dominate the thoughts of unbelievers, but your heavenly Father already knows all your needs.'"

The God Who created us with those needs certainly knows how necessary they are. But Jesus makes us this promise: "'Seek the Kingdom of God above all else, and live righteously, and he will give you everything you need'" (Matt. 6:33).

Do I spend too much time decorating my home? Or am I wasting time on social media? Do I spend hours just amusing myself? Is the clock ticking away the time while I am keeping up with the times? Have I been busy doing other things, instead of loving my family, nurturing them, caring for others in need, doing God's work? May God help all of us to seriously seek God's kingdom before all else and trust Him to provide our every need—just as He promised.

6
Like Sheep Needing a Shepherd

It really is an emerald isle, I thought as our plane circled to land in Dublin, Ireland. Its beautiful green pastures seemed to beckon a welcome to a land of tranquility. But it suddenly didn't seem very tranquil when we landed and had to wade through a solution of disinfectant, with our shoes on, because hoof and mouth disease was devastating Irish cattle.

In our rental car, driving toward the legendary Hill of Tara, we were stopped by a great herd of sheep crowding the narrow road, milling about, bleating piteously. The sheep on the fringes of the flock darted into the middle, roiling the flock and driving others into the deep ditches beside the road. Little lambs nudged the ewes, frantically seeking their own mothers. Why was that flock there, lacking food and water and in obvious danger? Where was their careless shepherd?

It was impossible to drive through them. We waited while the flock churned around us. An old Irishman ambled by. We rolled down a window.

"Why are these sheep here?" we asked.

He took his pipe out of his mouth, spit, and then said in his thick Irish brogue, "A quarrel between the man who owns the pasture and the man who rents it for his flock. Drove them out. No place for them to go."

When we returned that afternoon, the sheep were still milling in the roadway, bleating, frantic with anxiety.

This morning, as I read Matthew 9:35-39, I remembered that flock of distraught sheep.

Jesus traveled through all the towns and villages of that area, teaching in the synagogues and announcing the Good News about the Kingdom. And he healed every kind of disease and illness. When he saw the crowds, he had compassion on them because they were confused and helpless, like sheep without a shepherd. He said to his disciples, "The harvest is great, but the workers are few. So pray to the Lord who is in charge of the harvest; ask him to send more workers into his fields."

Is that how you feel right now? Are you weary and tired? Are you threatened by the unknown? Are you walking in a dark valley, not knowing where to turn?

Then you need Jesus, the Good Shepherd. Remember the familiar passage of Psalm 23? There, Jesus offers you green pastures and quiet waters. He promises to protect you from every danger. And because Jesus, your Good Shepherd, gave His life for you, He can guarantee you that "goodness and mercy shall follow" you through every step of life. He will protect you even when you must go "through the valley of the shadow of death." And then the Good Shepherd will bring you to rest and safety at last in the Father's fold.

After a day of sightseeing, we went back to our bed-and-breakfast in Dublin and asked our host about the welfare of that flock of sheep.

He smiled and said, "They worked it out. The sheep are back in the fold where they belong."

Come to your loving Shepherd, poor wandering lamb, distraught, not knowing where to turn. He's waiting for you with pity and love. "He said, 'They are my very own people. Surely they will not betray me again.' And he became their Savior. In all their suffering he also suffered, and he personally rescued them. In his love and mercy he redeemed them. He lifted them up and carried them through all the years" (Isa. 63:8-9).

1
If You Pay the Danes to Go Away

In the tenth century, the Saxon king Ethelred II, "the Unready," thought he'd get rid of Danish invaders by paying them what they asked. His nickname, "the Unready," meant he was ill-advised; and so it turned out because, of course, the Danes came back again and again for more loot!

British Prime Minister Neville Chamberlain thought he'd appease Hitler in 1938 by conceding Czechoslovakia to him, thinking to prevent war and bring about peace. As we well know, that did not stop Hitler from coveting more lands.

I remember a man who had lost his family because of his drinking. With compassionate hearts, Walt and I went to his home to try to help him.

In answer to our offer to help, the man filled a glass with liquor, held it up, and said to us, "Endgate! This is the last glass I'll ever drink."

But five "endgates" later, he was too drunk to speak coherently. Conceding even a small point to the enemy only increases his appetite and brings him back for more. Proverbs 14:12 says, "There is a path before each person that seems right, but it ends in death.."

What does that have to do with you and me? It's a reminder that we cannot yield to any proposal that nibbles at our integrity. Every day, the headlines tell us of someone who thought they could get by with a small infraction and yield just a tiny bit of their integrity but found the coils that entangled them were too great to break.

It isn't always easy to distinguish a proper compromise. In Matthew 5:25, Jesus said, "'When you are on the way to court with your adversary, settle your differences quickly.'" When the other person is right, then, of course, you agree with him. Proverbs 19:20 urges, "Get all the advice and instruction you can, so you will be wise the rest of your life."

When it is plainly a matter of right or wrong, we must never concede, never appease. If we can find a way to make the truth palatable to others, we certainly ought to try. If we can help others see how they will profit from choosing the right, we should. But let's never pay the Danes to go away, for they certainly will come back for more.

We will never have to make a choice that will dishonor our Creator. First Corinthians 10:31 says, "Whether you eat or drink, or whatever you do, do it all for the glory of God." What a wonderful path is laid before us! No matter our specific job description, we can honor God in our work every day.

8
Tomorrow Will Come

Do you remember when you were a child how very long it took for your birthday to come again? Later in life, I've discovered, birthdays seem to come too soon. But it is true: tomorrow will come. And the question I'm asking myself is whether when tomorrow comes, I will be truly glad or rather meet it with remorse and sadness? It depends, of course, on whether I did yesterday what I should have done.

Lord Chesterfield wrote his son, "Know the true value of time; snatch, seize, and enjoy every moment of it. No idleness, no laziness, no procrastination: never put off till tomorrow what you can do today." The things we postpone are important, essential for our welfare or the welfare of others but so difficult that we postpone them.

Hebrews 3:12-15 says:

> Be careful then, dear brothers and sisters. Make sure that your own hearts are not evil and unbelieving, turning you away from the living God. You must warn each other every day, while it is still "today," so that none of you will be deceived by sin and hardened against God. For if we are faithful to the end, trusting God just as firmly as when we first believed, we will share in all that belongs to Christ. Remember what it says: "Today when you hear his voice, don't harden your hearts as Israel did when they rebelled."

The wonderful truth about today and tomorrow is that today, you can do what God wants you to do. Today, you can call the friend from whom you've been estranged. Today, you can begin to break the bad habit that has frustrated you and your family. Today, you can do the task you've postponed because you were afraid to try. Today, you can write the letter you should have written yesterday. Today, you can encourage the fellow worker next to you. Today, you can listen to your child grieving for more of your attention. Today, you can affirm your spouse of your deep love. But you need to do it today, not postpone it again until tomorrow.

There's another wonderful truth about today and tomorrow: the Scriptures assure us that nothing—*nothing*—can separate us from the love of God—nothing past and nothing future.

> And I am convinced that nothing can ever separate us from God's love. Neither death nor life, neither angels nor demons, neither our fears for today nor our worries about tomorrow— not even the powers of hell can separate us from God's love. No power in the sky above or in the earth below—indeed, nothing in all creation will ever be able to separate us from the love of God that is revealed in Christ Jesus our Lord." (Rom. 8:38-39).

Thank God that He has given us today to do what He wants us to do. And thank God that all of our tomorrows are also in His powerful, unchanging, loving hands. We need not fear tomorrow when we trust God. And today, with His grace and wisdom, we can do what He wants us to do.

9
Out of Quarantine

With the advances made in inoculations, diphtheria is not the virulent threat it once was. But when I was a nine-year-old child, the diagnosis was extremely serious. No one knew how I'd been exposed to it; but when the doctor came to the house, he told my parents, "It's diphtheria. This child will be dead tomorrow if she does not get the antitoxin now."

I got the shot, of course, but then the whole family was quarantined for three weeks. I was isolated in a back bedroom and bathroom and did not see a human face for three weeks, except for the county nurse who came occasionally to check on me. Meals were put on a tray and left by the door. Mother did her heart-rending best to keep me comfortable and entertained with paper dolls and modeling clay and books, but it was a lonely and fearful time in my life.

One wonderful day, my exile finally ended. I remember walking out of that prison-like room out onto the porch, breathing the sweet, warm Texan air, seeing with new eyes the beautiful azure sky and green grass, reveling in the smiling faces of my dear family. Oh, what joy welled up in my heart!

But then my big sister said, "Mother, Libby hasn't washed a dish for three weeks. She ought to have to wash all the dishes today!" (As you can guess, she didn't like washing dishes very much!)

Well, she was right. I hadn't washed a dish for three weeks. Suddenly, the sky darkened. The air was hot and sticky.

But Mother said, "No, Grace. No dishes for Libby today. She can do anything she wants to do today. She's free."

Something like that has happened to us. We were all infected with the virulent disease of sin. It threatened not just our joy and peace, but also our eternal welfare as well. Then Jesus, the Great Physician, offered us redemption for free, guaranteed forever. What a delight!

But Satan, who, the Bible says, prowls around trying to find someone he can rob of joy, whispers, "Oh, you think it's that simple, do you? Well, it isn't. You've got a great stack of stuff to do before you are really free." The day darkens, and our joy is gone.

But then the Lord Jesus says, "Enough, Satan! Get out. This is my child, and I've already finished the work. There's not a thing more needed." Romans 8:1 confirms, "So now there is no condemnation for those who belong to Christ Jesus." Christ's work is done. He's paid the price, and we are free.

10
I Will Bring Joy to This Office

A friend of mine is the head of a government agency. Recently, she interviewed an applicant for a position in her office. She seemed to have good qualifications and the kind of personality that would work well with other employees. Then the woman being interviewed said confidently, "I will bring joy to this office."

Is joy needed in an office? Yes, conflict between employees handicaps everyone. It's difficult to keep your mind on your work if others have a defensive attitude, if they are busy protecting their "rights," or if they push for their own private agenda. No office needs a "drama queen"! Proverbs 15:23 says, "Everyone enjoys a fitting reply; it is wonderful to say the right thing at the right time!"

The next obvious question is when the employee got the job, did she bring the joy to the office? The answer, again, is yes. The joy she brings is not an artificial, Pollyanna kind of optimism. She isn't flippant. The welfare of many depends on how well she does her work. She looks for ways to enable others to do their job. She respects them. She enjoys doing her own work with accuracy and speed. Others are not kept waiting for her.

That kind of attitude doesn't come from denying reality. It comes from the assurance that no matter what the circumstances are, an employee can do God's will. How can you be sure this is true? Romans 14:4 says, "Who are you to condemn someone else's servants? Their own master will judge whether they stand or fall. And with the Lord's help, they will stand and receive his approval." We have God's assurance that He will help you do as you should.

From where does this kind of resolute joy come? It is not necessarily from the job or its income. Most jobs have boring and distasteful aspects. Even Queen Elizabeth must have sometimes tired of "queening."

The Bible offers a unique answer. The story is told in the book of Nehemiah. The Israelites had come back from slavery in Babylon. They faced the daunting job of rebuilding their destroyed homes. They were tired and discouraged. Nehemiah gathered them together to read the Scriptures. As they heard those precious words, they began to weep. Nehemiah said, "Don't be dejected and sad, for the joy of the Lord is your strength!" (Neh. 8:10).

Real joy comes from knowing the Lord. His joy will give you the strength to bring joy wherever you are, whatever your task. So yes, you can say with confidence, "I will bring joy to this office."

Couldn't a mother bring that kind of joy into her home? Couldn't an old man in assisted living, even with his physical difficulties, bring joy into his contacts with others? Couldn't someone in the healthcare business, with all the sad situations with which they have to cope, still say, "I will bring joy into this job"? Couldn't a student in a noisy classroom still bring joy to other students? Couldn't I—no matter how I earn my living, no matter the pressures I feel— say, "I will bring joy in this place"? Yes, you can because the joy of the Lord is my strength. God promised it.

11
Does Your Saw Need Sharpening?

Stephen Covey, in his book on habits, says that habit number seven, "Sharpen the Saw," is the habit which makes the other six effective. He tells the story of a logger who spent five hours trying to cut down a huge tree. But his saw blade was dull.

"Why don't you sharpen your saw?" an experienced logger asked.

"I don't have time to sharpen my saw. I'm in a terrible hurry."

Well, duh![1]

You and I can see the flaw in his thinking. But sometimes, we can't see, in our own lives, that we are working with dull tools. Is it time to step back, both at work and at home, to analyze our goals and the tools we need to sharpen to achieve those goals?

Are unimportant interruptions draining my time? Is there a better way to accomplish this task? Do I need to gain a skill? Should I take a refresher course? Have I lost my true goal of serving others in my drive to finish a task?

Wise King Solomon said, "If the iron be blunt, and he do not whet the edge, then must he put to more strength: but wisdom is profitable to direct" (Eccl. 10:10). If your work seems to be heavy and you feel you are having to use too much strength, perhaps your blade needs sharpening!

Perhaps you need to pray, as you consider your work at the beginning of each day, "Lord, who do You want me to help today? A fellow worker who is

---

1   Stephen R. Covey, *The 7 Habits of Highly Effective People* (Los Angeles: Free Press, 2004).

struggling? A client who needs encouragement? Lord, let my blade be sharp and useful today."

12
Accountable for Our Silences

When I was a child, I worried about the Scripture that says we are accountable for our "idle word[s]" (Matt. 12:36). I thought maybe it meant I wasn't ever supposed to tell a joke! Now I realize it means I will be held to the same standard I impose on others. But Benjamin Franklin says something just as sobering: "As we are accountable for our words, so we are also accountable for our silences."

Proverbs 31:8-9 says, "Speak up for those who cannot speak for themselves; ensure justice for those being crushed. Yes, speak up for the poor and helpless, and see that they get justice."

When I think of people who have spoken up for those who cannot speak for themselves, I think of Harriet Beecher Stowe. She was married to an impoverished, dreaming college professor. She suffered ill health much of her life. She had seven children and not only had to feed them but also needed to weave the cloth to make their clothes, wash their clothes in a tub over a fire in the backyard, and even build their furniture, while trying to write simple stories to help pay their bills.

They lived in Cincinnati in the 1850s, just across the Ohio River from Kentucky, a slave state. Harriet experienced firsthand the sorrow and burdens of slavery and grieved because she didn't know how to help.

Her sister-in-law wrote her, "Hattie, if I could use a pen as you can, I would write something to make this nation feel what an accursed thing slavery is."

When Harriet read this, she rose from her chair, crushed the letter in her hand, and said, "I will write something! I will, if I live."

What she wrote was *Uncle Tom's Cabin*. It was her poignant plea for "those who cannot speak for themselves." It stirred the hearts of people who had been silent too long.[2] May God help us not to be silent when we ought to speak!

---

2   Harriet Beecher Stowe, *Life of Harriet Beecher Stowe: Compiled From Her Letters and Journals by Her Son Charles Edward Stowe* (Independently published, 2016).

13
Little Is Much

It's almost a fairy tale—the love story of Kittie Jenneth and Fred Suffield. She had a lovely contralto voice and in the 1900s was training for the concert stage in busy New York City. Kittie took a train from New York headed for Ottawa. At that time, Fred was in his cabin in the Canadian wilderness, riding out a terrific snowstorm.

A frantic knocking on his door revealed a man, desperate and cold. He'd come from a train stalled by the blizzard, and now the passengers were about to freeze to death. He'd risked his life to try to find help and saw Fred's lighted cabin. Immediately, Fred grabbed a lantern and escorted all of the passengers to his small cabin for refuge until help could come. Kittie was one of his grateful guests. She wrote him a thank-you letter. He responded; she wrote back; and you can guess the rest of that story!

After they married, they heard the gospel in A. J. Shea's church in Ottawa and gave their lives to the Lord Jesus. They began an itinerant preaching ministry, going from community to community, she singing and playing the piano and he preaching. They invited Pastor Shea's young son to come with them for a week's meeting to help in the services. But when he stood to sing, his voice cracked; and in tears, he vowed he'd never sing again.

"The trouble is the song was too high for you. Let me play it for you in a lower key," she said reasonably. She smiled and played, and he sang—and that young man kept on singing for the rest of his life until he died when he was 104 years old. You've heard of him: George Beverly Shea, who, they tell us, sang before more people in his lifetime than anyone else in the world ever had.

At a celebration of George Beverly Shea's life, he sang "Little Is Much when God Is in It." People were puzzled. Why would Shea choose such an unfamiliar song? Kittie Suffield had written the words and music. Kittie was the unknown, unacclaimed person who, at a crossroads in George Beverly Shea's life, helped him make a decision that not only altered his life but also brought the gospel to millions.[3]

I can't even find a picture of Kittie; I've told you all that seems to be known about her (except that she was buried by her husband in Forest Lawn Cemetery in Los Angeles in 1972). How eloquently does her life demonstrate that wherever God has put you, whatever job you must do, no matter your seeming success or failures, if you do it in obedience to Him, your task is essential to His kingdom.

In Mark 9:41, Jesus said something so startling, we can hardly believe it's true. But it is! May this truth give you great joy today as you work, even if it seems at an insignificant, unrewarding task: "For whosoever shall give you a cup of water to drink in my name, because ye belong to Christ, verily, I say unto you, he shall not lose his reward" (Mark 9:41).

---

3   Bill H., "Kittie Suffield – 'Little is Much, When God is in it,'" *Church History Minute Notes,* October 14, 2018, https://bill8147.blogspot.com/2018/10/kittie-suffield-little-is-much-when-god.html.

14
Could She Speak Truth and Save the Friendship?

She was a dear, young girl, and her aunt (a friend of mine) was troubled because she was about to marry a young man the aunt knew was not yet ready for marriage. Beverly[4] was a trusted friend of the young man as well, and she yearned to help him in this time of life-altering decision. She felt he was perhaps too self-centered to be taking on the responsibilities of a home and family so soon.

Should she tell her niece about her reservations? If she did, would the niece find it unforgivable? Could she speak the truth and still have the intimate relationship with her that she'd enjoyed through the years? Would the young man be angered that she'd intervened? Was it even her business, Beverly wondered guiltily, to interfere in the lives of these two young people she loved so much?

"Well, yes," she decided, "I must. I have a responsibility to them both. But I'll ask the Lord to help me know exactly what to say and when to shut up. I love these two kids too much to hurt them. God, help me to speak the truth and still save our friendship!"

She did talk to each of them, separately. Nevertheless, they went ahead with their wedding plans. Undaunted, Beverly played the organ at the wedding and sent them on their way with a joyous recessional. And of course, because she loved them, she prayed for them.

---

4   Name changed to protect privacy.

It turned out her misgivings were well-founded. The young man was immature. He found it hard to think unselfishly in order to keep the vows he'd made before God. But since Beverly had been careful not to destroy the friendship while offering her advice, she was able to help them handle their conflicts. That friendship deepened through the years, and they thanked her again and again for "speak[ing] the truth in love" (Eph. 4:15) when they really needed it.

Ephesians 4:14-15 says, "Then we will no longer be immature like children. We won't be tossed and blown about by every wind of new teaching. We will not be influenced when people try to trick us with lies so clever they sound like the truth. Instead, we will speak the truth in love, growing in every way more and more like Christ, who is the head of his body, the church." "Speaking truth" without love will sound like jangling, critical noise. Truth can't be heard above the dissonance.

But love that doesn't "speak the truth" isn't true love at all. It's a kind of self-love that craves to be "liked," rather than valuing the welfare of the one we say we love. Not easily done, is it, to speak difficult truth but with so much love that a friendship is saved? Beverly would tell you that it is certainly worth the risk. The lives of two young people were forever blessed because she dared to speak the truth with profound love.

15
What's That in Your Hand?

Walt and I enjoyed an intriguing story in this week's Bible reading. Exodus 4:1-5 tells how God had a job for Moses to do—an immense, history-changing job for him to accomplish. But Moses kept objecting: "I'm not smart enough." "Nobody will listen to me." "I'm tongue-tied." "You know I can't do it."

Then God said, "Moses, what do you have in your hand?"

"A stick."

"That's what I'm going to use to deliver your nation from bondage."

"A stick?"

"Yes, a stick."

It reminded me of an incident years ago. Walt and I were driving back home from New York in our Volkswagen Microbus. It was after midnight, and we were on I-85 at the Gaffney exit when the engine started sputtering.

"It's the distributor," Walt decided.

We sputtered into town, hoping we might find a service station open, knowing it was really too late for anything to be open. Sure enough, everything was closed!

The engine died. Walt went to the back, opened the engine compartment, and took off the distributor cap. Sure enough, one of the breaker points had burned off. (This was in the '60s, before the sophistication of computers and micro-tolerances in engines.) He surveyed his resources, decided a paperclip I offered him might work, and jerry-rigged it; and we limped on home.

It may be, in some areas of your life, that you are feeling like Moses. You see the great challenge ahead, and you know how important it is. But you may feel inadequate to meet it. Then God asks, "What do you have in your hand?" What you find in your hand is what He is going to do to help you accomplish the task He has laid on you. This is true whether your challenge is child-rearing, inter-personal relationships, finances, or skills required by your job. You can do what God wants you to do today because He takes the responsibility for equipping you when He assigns the job. And you won't have to settle for paperclips to take care of it!

Today, you can accomplish what God wants you to do. He will give you the wisdom, the skills, and the joy you need to do it. So today, let's claim His help in doing what we find in our hands to do.

16
Sometimes I Ask God "Why?"

Okay, I'll admit it right away: sometimes when I ask God why, it's really a stupid question with an obvious answer; and I shouldn't have had to ask.

When I was a little girl, our family read aloud a chapter from the Bible every day. We were in the book of Proverbs and came to Proverbs 14:12 (KJV): "There is a way which seemeth right unto a man, but the end thereof are the ways of death."

Rather than being struck by the obvious warning in the verse (and probably being a little smart-alecky), I said to God, "How come, God, You don't know good English? 'End' is a single subject, and 'are' is a plural verb; subject and verb are supposed to agree!"

Later, I learned that God gave us His Word in Hebrew and Greek. Somebody had translated that verse into English. Furthermore, I learned about a "compound subject," which takes a plural verb. So much for that silly question.

Several years later, sitting on the front porch at night, looking up at the bright Texas stars, I said to God, "God, You're so big and great, why don't You know how hard it is to be a little ten-year-old girl with so many problems?"

Then I found Hebrews 4:14-16 in my Bible:

> So then, since we have a great High Priest who has entered heaven, Jesus the Son of God, let us hold firmly to what we believe. This High Priest of ours understands our weaknesses, for he faced all of the same testings we do, yet he did not sin. So let us come boldly to the throne of our gracious God. There we

will receive his mercy, and we will find grace to help us when we need it most.

My question was answered!

Now, sometimes, the questions I want God to answer are not trivial. They are visceral and heart-shredding, about undeniable loss.

"Oh, dear Lord, why did you take Tim away from us?"

Tim was our first-born grandson, an ardent Christian, a committed husband and father of two little girls, an enthusiastic and competent worker. He died two days after his thirty-sixth birthday, shortly after a stem-cell transplant for a rare blood disease. We loved him; and suddenly, he was gone. Why did God take away such a treasure?

But God knows me very well; and He knew that even if He told me why He had taken Tim, I would not understand. His wisdom, His love, and His strength are all beyond my human understanding. So in answering my why, He only said, "Oh, how great are God's riches and wisdom and knowledge! How impossible it is for us to understand his decisions and his ways!" (Rom. 11:33).

So what should I do when my heart is breaking and I don't understand what God is doing? Here's what King David decided to do: "Lord, my heart is not proud; my eyes are not haughty. I don't concern myself with matters too great or too awesome for me to grasp. Instead, I have calmed and quieted myself, like a weaned child who no longer cries for its mother's milk. Yes, like a weaned child is my soul within me. O Israel, put your hope in the Lord—now and always" (Psalm 131:1-3).

A baby nestled in his mother's arms doesn't ask questions. His mother holds him, and that's enough. He snuggles and rests. And that's what the Lord told me to do when I had questions I could not answer: just trust Him. He is dependable. He is wise. And He loves me.

17
If I Would Lead, I Must Serve

Years ago, the company I worked for hired a new office manager. Our CEO was aging; he hoped this new man would eventually take his place. Our CEO planned a beautiful day's retreat for the whole staff in the mountains, so we could get acquainted with our new boss. The new office manager made an affable, casual speech about how glad he was to be with us, how he looked forward to helping us become our very best in our tasks, how he felt his leadership qualities fit exactly into what our company needed. But at lunch, when we lined up at the various food bars, he ignored those waiting in line and moved to the front of each line to get his food. (We employees would have been glad to invite him to come to the front of the lines if he'd given us a chance. We'd have liked to make a good impression on our new boss!)

In the afternoon, we did a craft project. We could all work at our own pace, with all the tools we needed, except for one last bit, which required taking the project to a colleague with a little machine that would fasten it all together. As we completed our project, we stood patiently in the long line for that last finishing touch. Again, when the new office manager finished his, he stepped to the front of the line to have his handled first.

The Scriptures tell an interesting story about Jesus' twelve disciples as they were walking down a road together toward Capernaum. Mark 9:33-34 says, "After they arrived at Capernaum and settled in a house, Jesus asked his disciples, 'What were you discussing out on the road?' But they didn't answer, because they had been arguing about which of them was the greatest."

I don't blame the disciples for staying quiet! I wouldn't want to have to tell Jesus I'd been bragging on how great I was! The story continues in verse 35: "He sat down, called the twelve disciples over to him, and said, 'Whoever wants to be first must take last place and be the servant of everyone else.'" If I hope to be a good and successful leader, then I must do it by looking for ways to serve those I lead, rather than expecting them to serve me. The dear Lord Jesus, God Himself, set the example. Jesus is the very Son of God and Creator of the universe. But on the evening before He would die for us, He took off His robe, took a basin and a towel, and washed the dirty feet of each one of His disciples.

Don't let the familiarity of the story lessen the profound truth: if we would be great, if we would be a leader, then we must humble ourselves to serve the people we lead. Philippians 2:5-8 says, "You must have the same attitude that Christ Jesus had. Though he was God,-he did not think of equality with God as something to cling to. Instead, he gave up his divine privileges; he took the humble position of a slave and was born as a human being. When he appeared in human form, he humbled himself in obedience to God and died a criminal's death on a cross.

May God give me a heart to serve with the same attitude that Jesus had!

18
He Was a Bully, and He Frightened Me

I was a shy and awkward eleven-year-old girl in the sixth grade at James Bowie School. He was a gangly seventh grader. He chased me home after school every day to "give me a kiss." He was a bully, and he frightened me.

I coped the best I could. I lingered in the hallways for an hour after school. I changed the route I took home. I clustered with friends walking home. So far, I had escaped his clutches. But I knew some day, he was going to catch me alone.

So I went to my father. He wasn't a big man, but he was a Texan; and Texas men aren't afraid of anything—at least that was what this very-much-afraid child believed. I grew up hearing the true story of the Texas ranger sent to quell a riot in Fort Worth. He was met at the train by the frightened sheriff.

"Where are the rest of your men?" he asked. "You didn't come alone, did you?"

The Texas ranger drawled, "Sure, I'm alone. You have only one riot, don't you?"

I thought my daddy as fearless as that Texas ranger. He'd stop that kid from threatening me!

"Daddy, I need you to help me. This boy keeps chasing me home, wanting to kiss me. Please make him stop."

Instead, my father looked me squarely in the eyes. I wanted him to protect me, but he wanted me to learn to stand up for myself.

"Get yourself a big stick," he said quietly. "And if he tries to kiss you, hit him as hard as you can."

"Even if he's bigger than me?"

"Yes. Get a *big* stick. That will stop him. If it doesn't, I'll take care of him."

The next day, I went home from school through an alley to get away from the bully. But he followed me. A long tree branch lay on the ground at my feet. It was too big and heavy for me to wield, but I picked up the end of it.

"Go away, or I'm going to hit you with this," I said, my voice trembling in spite of myself.

He ran. He never bothered me again.

Daddy was right. There's no satisfaction in being a bully unless you see answering terror in the eyes of the one you are bullying.

You understand, if my big stick hadn't stopped the boy from harassing me, my brave father would have taken care of me. But Daddy knew I needed to learn how to stand up against bullying always, no matter who it is bullying me. No matter their status or influence, no matter how unimportant the bullied person may feel, threatening someone who cannot defend themselves is dead wrong. It has to be stopped. Confrontation is the only answer.

But there are many weak and helpless people in our society, people who have no recourse to get away, no alternative. They have no resources. If they lose their job, their children starve. They can't hit back. Their very helplessness inflames the bully. God says it is our responsibility to watch out for those who can't protect themselves and do whatever is necessary to protect them. "Brothers and sisters, we urge you to warn those who are lazy. Encourage those who are timid. Take tender care of those who are weak. Be patient with everyone. See that no one pays back evil for evil, but always try to do good to each other and to all people" (1 Thess. 5:14-15).

Can you remember how it feels to be threatened and frightened? Then "encourage those who are timid" and "take tender care of those who are weak."

19
We're Not Given an Option

C. K. Chesterton wrote, "Forgiveness means forgiving the unforgivable, else it is not forgiveness at all."

Ouch! That hurts! See, it's easy for me to forgive some things: unimportant slights, unintentional barbs, pesky irritations. But if someone deliberately hurts my relationship with someone I love, if they tell an untruth that damages my reputation, or if they cause me severe financial loss, then it's a whole different matter. I find it very difficult to forgive.

But God reminds me that's when I must forgive. He tells me to forgive even my enemies because I desperately needed forgiveness from Him for all the things I did to hurt Him. I had wronged God far more than anyone has ever wronged me. Yet He, in His mercy, forgave me every single sin. "Be kind to each other, tenderhearted, forgiving one another, just as God through Christ has forgiven you." (Eph. 4:32).

I am not given an option. I must, with God's help, forgive those who wrong me—even if they hurt me deliberately, even if they don't apologize, even if they don't even care that they hurt me, even if they continue to try to harm me. After all, God has forgiven me.

20
What I Learned from a Cough Drop Wrapper

How come you always get sick when you're behind in your work? Why not get sick only when you're caught up at work? What you certainly don't need when you aren't feeling well is a lecture on how much better you ought to be performing!

That's the way I felt the other day. I thought a cough drop would soothe a scratchy throat. But as I unwrapped it, I saw little pithy statements printed all over the wrapper.

"Don't try harder. Do harder!"

"Take charge and mean it."

"Don't give up on yourself!"

"Dust off and get up."

That's not exactly what I want to hear from a cough drop wrapper when I'm feeling tired and my work's not caught up. And then I remember a wonderful message Jesus gave us about work and our weaknesses. He said, "'Come to me, all of you who are weary and carry heavy burdens, and I will give you rest. Take my yoke upon you. Let me teach you, because I am humble and gentle at heart, and you will find rest for your souls. For my yoke is easy to bear, and the burden I give you is light'" (Matt. 11:28-30).

That's what I need to remember. When I am feeling "weary," I need to run to Jesus and take His yoke. But isn't a yoke what they use on a pair of oxen to make them pull a load? Yes, but notice what Jesus is promising here. He invites us to join Him in His yoke, so His strength will carry our burdens. Yes, we have work to do; but when Jesus is working with us, we will find His yoke "easy" and His burden "light."

Now about that cough drop wrapper: suppose the Smith Brothers still make cough drops?

21
Turn Off the Hose

We Texans celebrate Christmas with fireworks. Don't ask me why; we just do. The whole family had come to the home place one year for Christmas, as we often did. We gathered in the dusk as the men in the family lit their noisy fireworks. The grandchildren oohed and aahed on cue.

Then one of the dying, glowing embers floated to the roof of the house. Daddy ran into the house to get a pitcher of water. Mother, the ardent grower of all green things, knew where the outside faucet for the hose was; so she ran and turned it on. Just as she raised the hose toward the roof, Daddy charged through the door with pitcher in hand. Mother's strong spray of water hit him full in the face.

Mother, almost as if she were paralyzed with surprise, held the hose on him. He stood stock still in the doorway, as if he, too, was too surprised to move. (Actually, our dear, mild-mannered mother may have held it on him a few minutes longer than really necessary! But then, that was part of the fun of the holidays, wasn't it?) And we laughed even harder when we realized that the vagrant wisp of ember on the roof had long since quietly expired without a bit of threat to the home.

How often does that happen in ordinary life? Do I complain about the credit card balance increasing month by month and struggle to pay the minimum amount? Wouldn't it be better to admit to myself that I don't really need all the stuff I keep charging to the account and stop the spending? Shouldn't I turn off the faucet instead of just mopping up the water?

Do I stay irritated about a relationship, tired of the constant bickering and conflict? Wouldn't it be better to turn off the flow of hurtful opinions I think I have a right to express? Couldn't I let minor disagreements dissolve instead of ramping them up?

Do I reprimand my children because they leave their innumerable toys strewn about the house? Should I perhaps keep fewer toys within their reach and remind them, just before bedtime, to stow them all away in a convenient toy box?

Shouldn't I carefully search for a solution to a problem at work instead of just hoping it will go away? Why do I postpone a decision while treating the symptoms instead of the cause? Why do I concentrate on mopping up the water instead of turning off the hose?

King Solomon warns, in Proverbs 4:23, "Guard your heart above all else, for it determines the course of your life." Oh, God, may I know my own heart so well that I address the root causes of my problems, rather than simply dealing with the outfall of my unguarded thoughts!

22
Showing Mercy with Cheerfulness

You've often found yourself in the same kind of situation. Someone needs help, and it's up to you to help them—but do you *have* to do it cheerfully, or can you grumble about it just a little bit, so they'll know how inconvenient it is?

A couple of weeks ago, our granddaughter in college called to ask Grandpa Handford's advice. She would have phoned her father, who keeps her car running well; but her father and mother were in California with her other grandmother, who was desperately ill.

"Grandpa, my car keeps running hot, and I have to keep putting water in the radiator every few miles. Will I ruin the car if I keep driving it hot?"

She really was just asking for advice, but her loving grandfather could hear the panic in her voice. "No, honey. Can you get over to our house? You can use my van until your daddy gets home."

It really wasn't such a big sacrifice. The two of us could juggle our schedules for a couple of days so we could get by with one automobile. But the couple of days turned into two weeks. There was a complication in getting the car running again.

Our granddaughter called again. "Grandpa, Daddy hasn't finished fixing my car. Do you need the van?"

Well, yes, he needed it. But the child had to have transportation. So it was a given that she could use his automobile. The only thing is, didn't she need to know how much of an inconvenience it was? But Grandpa could hear a Bible verse in his mind that says, "If you have a gift for showing kindness to others, do it gladly" (Rom. 12:8).

He certainly was going to show kindness to the child. And yes, he certainly needed to do it gladly.

"Do you need the van yet?" she asked cautiously.

"No, Christina," Grandpa said cheerfully, "we'll manage just fine." And we did. What a joy it was to us not to add to the burden of someone in need by weighing them down further with embarrassment and obligation.

23
How Small a Thing Can I Pray About?

When I start to pray and I remember that God is the infinite, incomparable Creator of the universe, I'm sometimes ashamed and embarrassed. Should I really bother Him with the petty, mundane problems that fill my life? Doesn't He have too much on his plate to worry about my trivial problems?

Corrie ten Boom, the indomitable Dutch woman who saved the lives of so many Jews during World War II, has a simple answer for that: "Any concern too small to be turned into a prayer is too small to be made into a burden."

In other words, if I think it's too unimportant to pray about, then it's too unimportant for me to worry about. But—and it's a wonderful *but*—God has something important to say about that. He Himself told us to "give all your worries and cares to God, for he cares about you" (I Peter 5:7). He wants all of it—every heavy, worrisome burden and every niggling little problem! We are told to throw all our cares on Jesus because He cares about us. He loves us so much that He was willing to endure the torments of crucifixion and death to redeem us from death. That's how much He cares. And since He is able to fix every burden, take care of every worry of ours, huge or tiny, He wants us to cast it on His loving heart. Because He cares about you, He cares about your burden; and He will take care of it for you. Don't carry around a burden too small to pray about.

24
God's Creation Can't Help but Praise Him

This morning's Bible reading in I Chronicles 16:31-34 was so remarkable, I was taken aback.

> Let the heavens be glad, and the earth rejoice! Tell all the nations, "The Lord reigns!" Let the sea and everything in it shout his praise! Let the fields and their crops burst out with joy! Let the trees of the forest sing for joy before the Lord, for he is coming to judge the earth. Give thanks to the Lord, for he is good! His faithful love endures forever.

In my surprise, I should have remembered Job 38:7; "As the morning stars sang together and all the angels shouted for joy." And Psalm 65:13 says, "The meadows are clothed with flocks of sheep, and the valleys are carpeted with grain. They all shout and sing for joy!" And the very last line of the book of Psalms says, "Let everything that breathes sing praises to the LORD!" (Psalm 150:6).

So I wondered. Can skies really "rejoice"? Can the earth itself actually "be glad"? Can the stars truly sing? Can a field of corn really shout for joy? For that matter, does my little dachshund Schatzi, who certainly does "have breath," actually praise the Lord? I think maybe she does. Sometimes, she asks with great urgency to go outside. But once out, she often forgets her urgency. She stands completely still for a moment or two, her head lifted, oblivious to her surroundings. I wonder if maybe she's praising the Lord.

I watch the little gray finch who rents the birdhouse outside my window. He sometimes flies in and out, busily feeding his squawking family. Sometimes, he perches quietly on the roof of his house and sings with all his heart. The little bird breathes, and he seems to praise the Lord.

I look back on a memorable morning drive across the Alps by way of the Brennan Pass, seeing a Swiss farmer let his calves out of the stable in the stone foundation of his house. They pranced out, leaping and cavorting. They seemed to be thanking God for the new day.

I remember watching two of our horses, united after a year's separation, nickering when they first glimpsed each other, and then racing, circling the pasture together, again and again. Were they thanking God they were together?

Have you seen dolphins dancing in the surf, leaping in elegant movements over and over again? I wonder if they also praise God as they play.

I remember standing in an Iowa field of corn in July, the stalks higher than my head, as I listened to them rustle in the wind. They had no voice, but they honored their Creator just by their rustle.

Why does the whole creation rejoice? Psalm 96:11-13 tells us why: "Let the heavens be glad, and the earth rejoice! Let the sea and everything in it shout his praise! Let the fields and their crops burst out with joy! Let the trees of the forest sing for joy before the LORD, for he is coming! He is coming to judge the earth. He will judge the world with justice, and the nations with his truth."

One wonderful day, the Lord Jesus will return and reclaim His marred creation. So we can thank Him and praise Him today, along with His beautiful creation, as we await that promised day of deliverance.

25
The Surprising Cure for My Bad Hair Day

My bad hair day began the day my long-time hairdresser told me she was retiring. And that bad hair day lasted for several weeks while I desperately shopped to replace her. My kids would tell you my hairdo is not just old-fashioned, it's Neanderthalic (think Princess Grace Kelly in the '50s).

I phoned the hair salons in my zip code and asked, "Do you have someone on staff who does a French twist?"

If they said, "What's that?" I said, "Nevermind. You don't."

But one hairdresser answered, "French twist? Certainly. Come on in. Ask for Barbara."

When I arrived, I found Barbara at her computer googling "French twist." That dear woman had never done a French twist but her "can-do" attitude charmed me. She eagerly met the challenge and felt confident she could master even my old-fashioned hairstyle. She is a joyful Christian and a devoted wife and mother; and she entertains me by wearing all kinds of beautiful clothes, different hairstyles, and bright straw hats. She has been God's good gift to me and the cure for my bad hair days. She's the sweet embodiment of Colossians 3:23-24: "Work willingly at whatever you do, as though you were working for the Lord rather than for people. Remember that the Lord will give you an inheritance as your reward, and that the Master you are serving is Christ."

I find that Scripture astounding. God says that whatever I'm doing, I'm to work hard and cheerfully because I'm working for Jesus. Some days, yes, I write a Bible study or counsel a woman burdened by cares. But many days, I am driven from task to task, meeting sudden emergencies, with no choice of control. I work at things I must do again tomorrow—serving a meal, scrubbing a toilet, picking up toys left by a child, counseling a friend. Could the Lord Jesus possibly look on those menial tasks as actually serving Him?

God says yes. Read it again. It's true, if you're a Christian—whether you're a project manager or a janitor, a used car salesman or a fashion designer, a mother or a father, a business owner or an employee. It might seem the most boring of tasks. But God says, "Do it well because you are doing it for Jesus' sake, not just for a paycheck. Your reward will be from the Lord Christ Himself."

If you really believed that, wouldn't it make a tremendous difference in how you viewed today's tasks? Wouldn't it make holy even the simplest of menial tasks? According to this Scripture, there is no difference between the value of what a pastor does and what a stenographer does when you are a child of God and do it to honor Him. There is no "secular" job; it's all "sacred" and valued by God when you set out to honor Him in your daily chores.

The sign in a beauty shop says, "I'm a beautician, not a magician." But Barbara's careful craftsmanship, her "can-do" attitude toward problems, and her sweet Christian spirit, did make my bad hair day magically disappear.

26
When You Have to Make a Hard Decision

Most choices in life are perhaps pretty simple. There's the right thing to do and the wrong thing to do, and the choice then is no choice at all: you simply do the right thing.

But sometimes there isn't an easy, obvious answer. Neither choice is intrinsically right or wrong. What you decide may affect the lives of others, for good or ill. The choice you make may affect your own financial and emotional security. Either choice may bring both good and bad results. To put further pressure on you, you may have an inexorable deadline.

I always knew when I saw my husband Walt with a yellow legal tablet in his hands, brooding with bowed head at his desk, he was considering the merits and liabilities of some important decision he was having to make. He'd draw a line down the middle of the page, label one column "pros" and the other column "cons." Under each heading, he would write down every conceivable effect of the decision, even the trivial ones. He would look long and carefully at each entry. And then I'd see him bow his head and ask God to give him the wisdom to make the right decision.

Sometimes the decision he made brought hardship with it (for nearly every decision of life certainly does have some hardship). When it did, he'd take out that yellow pad and read again the reasons he'd chosen that particular path, then take up his task again, reassured that God had led him aright.

What a comfort it is to know that God Himself wants to give you clear leading in life. Proverbs 3:5-6 says, "Trust in the Lord with all your heart; do not depend on your own understanding. Seek his will in all you do, and he will show you which path to take." This promise from God doesn't say that the path He led me on will have no obstacles, no bypasses, no conflict. It does promise me that the Holy God Who created me with such love will choose the best path for me and that He'll be by my side every step of the way.

I remember a time in my life when I was forced to make a truly huge decision, one that would affect the rest of my life. Although I prayed all night about it, I had no assurance of which choice was right. In the morning, I made the decision the best I could and caught the train that would take me on a difficult and lonely journey. It ended well. (Someday, I'll tell you the story of how I met my Prince Charming at the end of that lonely journey.)

I honestly had no assurance the morning I caught that train that I had made the right choice. But I did have God's assurance that He would not let me make a wrong choice when I honestly wanted to do right. Isaiah 50:10 says, "Who among you fears the Lord and obeys his servant? If you are walking in darkness, without a ray of light, trust in the Lord and rely on your God." Sometimes, when we've asked the Lord for guidance in a decision, we may still not see how it is going to work out right. We will still "walk in darkness and have no light." What must we do then? Trust in the name of the Lord and rely on your God! Simple and comforting. When we look to God for guidance in our decision-making, He will give it, no matter how we might feel.

27
Solitude in a Noisy World

My son John rides his cherry-red Pacific Coast Honda up into the mountains once in a while. The other day, I asked him why it was so appealing.

"The solitude," he answered. "I can hear God talk to me."

Susanna Wesley didn't have that option in the eighteenth century. She was the mother of nineteen children. One of them, Charles, grew up to write many wonderful hymns we still sing in church today. His brother John grew up to conduct revivals and establish churches all over the British Isles. Historians say those revivals saved England from the kind of bloody revolution that destroyed France.

Susanna's husband was a busy pastor who took little time for his family. You can imagine how crowded Susanna's days must have been with nineteen children: washing clothes, weaving cloth, sewing garments, tending the garden, preparing meals, cleaning fireplaces, making candles, constructing furniture, teaching her children to read. Yet she felt her primary responsibility was the spiritual nurturing of her children. What did she do when she needed solitude? How could she hear God talk to her in such a noisy, demanding atmosphere? She simply threw her voluminous apron up over her head! When the children saw their mother's face hidden by her apron, they knew they needed to be very, very quiet. Mother wanted to be alone. She wanted to hear God talk to her.

The Bible tells us the story of the prophet Elijah, who ran all the way from Canaan down to Mount Sinai to escape wicked Queen Jezebel's plot to kill him. Here he felt absolutely abandoned by God. The story, told in 1 Kings

19:9-18, talks about a conversation God had with Elijah. But God didn't speak to him through the "mighty windstorm." He didn't speak to Elijah in the earthquake He sent or in the fire. Rather, the Scripture says, God talked to him in a "gentle whisper." Elijah heard that "gentle whisper" and gathered his courage to go back home to do what God had told him to do.

We long to hear God's voice—to know He's listening to us, that He cares about us, that He hasn't abandoned us. Why can't we hear Him? Perhaps because we live in such a raucous, boom-box kind of world, His voice is drowned out. That's why we need solitude. We need to set aside time to hear God's voice.

In Psalm 46:10, God says, "'Be still, and know that I am God.'" Be still. Be quiet. Turn off the incessant noise in your mind. Wait quietly. Listen. Then you will know that God is God and that He wants to have a quiet conversation with you. But it requires solitude. And we will have to work to find it. But oh, how wonderful it is when we hear Him talking to us and telling us what is on His heart!

28
Why Didn't You Come Sooner?

One of the first churches Walt pastored was a new small congregation in a western suburb of Chicago. We met each Sunday in an elementary school building in the neighborhood, and our people were having a wonderful time working together in constructing a building for our permanent church home. They were doing the work themselves, and the building progressed as we collected enough money for each step of the project.

Walt had been in Chicago; and on his way home, a highway detour sent him through a pleasant suburban neighborhood. As he drove down the unfamiliar road, he saw, on the curb in front of a home, a discarded hot water heater, placed there for sanitation workers to pick up on their weekly schedule.

Walt, his heart and mind always on the needs of the building construction, eyed the heater. *Hmm. We need a heating element for the baptistry water. Suppose the heating element in that thing still works?*

Normally, I think Walt would have been reluctant to barge into a strange home to ask for anything, but the needs of this church building project evidently overcame his natural reluctance. He rang the doorbell. An elderly gentleman answered it.

Walt blurted out the reason for his call. "Sir, I know this sounds crazy; but I'm a pastor in Glendale Heights, and we're building a new sanctuary. We need a heating element for the baptistry. Would you consider letting me have that water heater on your curb?"

"Why, please come in," the man answered. "We may have some other things to give you."

Stunned, Walt went in and spent a delightful time with the man and his wife, as they kept bringing out other things he might need for his new church building. Walt came to realize there was more than simple kindness in what they were doing. He sensed they had a spiritual hunger that only God can meet. So he told the them the blessed old story of how God loves the world and sent Jesus to make it so anyone who wants to can spend eternity in Heaven with Him.

They listened, rapt. The gospel may be "blessed" and "old" to us who have heard it again and again; but to these dear people, it was astonishingly new and overwhelming. Together, they bowed their heads and asked God for His gift of eternal salvation.

As Walt started to leave, loaded down with all the stuff they'd given him, the woman stopped him. With tears in her eyes, she said, "Walt, why didn't you come sooner? We've waited for this all our lives."

God's love may be a familiar and beloved story to you. God grant that you never lose the wonder of what it means. And God grant that we find the words to share His love with those we meet who hunger for it. Remember the words of Proverbs 24:11-12: "Rescue those who are unjustly sentenced to die; save them as they stagger to their death. Don't excuse yourself by saying, 'Look, we didn't know.' For God understands all hearts, and he sees you. He who guards your soul knows you knew. He will repay all people as their actions deserve."

29

Who Has the Most Important Job around Here?

Once in a while, I get to thinking I'm not very necessary for anything. So many of the tasks I do each day seem unimportant. Then I remember the tiny stapes bone, the smallest bone in the human body, and I feel better about the tasks God has assigned me. Sound complicated? It isn't, really.

I can't hear well. It has affected every part of my life. I can't hear what my children say. I hurt people's feelings because I misunderstand them. I dread public meetings because I can't hear, even with my hearing aids turned full volume.

I remember once sitting in chapel at Southside Christian School. I thought the principal asked me to go to the piano and play the introduction to the "Hallelujah Chorus." (Our students had just sung it in a Christmas program.) In front of the whole student body, in the very middle of the principal's message, I got up from the audience and went to the piano. But that wasn't at all what the principal had asked.

Don't even ask me about the time I thought my sister said she'd sprayed for fleas, when she had actually sprayed Febreze, an air freshener.

The ENT doctor told me that the little stapes bones in my middle ear had disintegrated from arthritis. Simply put, the stapes bone conducts the sound waves from the ear drum to the auditory nerve. (They're called stapes because they are shaped like a stirrup.) It was no wonder I couldn't hear. How could anything so tiny affect a human being's whole life? Believe me, they do!

And that's why the stapes bone comes to mind when I wonder if I am doing anything significant for God. The Lord Jesus says He has given every single one of us a task, an important task that no one but ourselves can accomplish. There are no unimportant people or unimportant jobs in the family of God. He has given each of us the job for which He designed us. First Corinthians 12:12-22 explains:

> The human body has many parts, but the many parts make up one whole body. So it is with the body of Christ. Some of us are Jews, some are Gentiles, some are slaves, and some are free. But we have all been baptized into one body by one Spirit, and we all share the same Spirit. Yes, the body has many different parts, not just one part. If the foot says, "I am not a part of the body because I am not a hand," that does not make it any less a part of the body. And if the ear says, "I am not part of the body because I am not an eye," would that make it any less a part of the body? If the whole body were an eye, how would you hear? Or if your whole body were an ear, how would you smell anything? But our bodies have many parts, and God has put each part just where he wants it. How strange a body would be if it had only one part! Yes, there are many parts, but only one body. The eye can never say to the hand, "I don't need you." The head can't say to the feet, "I don't need you." In fact, some parts of the body that seem weakest and least important are actually the most necessary.

That settles it, doesn't it? Each of us has a unique task to do for God today, right where we are! There are no unimportant people or unimportant jobs in the sight of our loving Heavenly Father.

30
Broken Things

I have an exquisite Aynsley English tea cup with a broken handle. It's broken, so why don't I throw it away? After all, I have a cupboard full of unbroken cups. Why not trash it and use a good cup?

I keep this cup because it is precious to me. My pastor's wife gave it to Walt and me for a wedding gift way back in 1948. I keep it because it's beautiful to me. The delicate and unusual shape of the saucer, the pretty flowers, and the gold rim all combine to make it beautiful. It pleases me. I keep it because it is still useful. A cup of tea tastes warm and sweet, even if I hold it with half a handle. And I keep it, especially, because it reminds me that though I am flawed and broken, chipped and faded, my dear Heavenly Father loves me and enjoys taking care of me.

Psalm 103:13-14 says, "The Lord is like a father to his children, tender and compassionate to those who fear him. For he knows how weak we are; he remembers we are only dust."

God looks at all of us broken, damaged people like a father who takes his little boy in his arms after the child has had a melt-down. That father isn't surprised the child is easily angered, easily frustrated. And he comforts and reassures his son that he still belongs in the family. Sure, he'll teach the child and reprimand him when he needs it, but his loving arms are always opened wide for comfort.

The father remembers that God made both him and his child out of the dirt of the ground. Genesis 2:7 says, "Then the LORD God formed the man from the dust of the ground. He breathed the breath of life into the man's nostrils, and the man became a living person."

God isn't surprised or disappointed when we fail, when we are rude or deceitful, when we put our own needs and desires above those for whom we should be caring. He knows that we are dust. Psalm 136:23 says it this way: "He remembered us in our weakness. *His faithful love endures forever.*" And He can forgive us because His dear Son gave His life for our redemption.

If God is so gracious and so kind to us in our brokenness, shouldn't we reflect that grace toward other people who are also flawed and broken? Is it right for us to hold a higher standard for others than we are able to reach ourselves? Should we trash someone who, in a moment of weakness, failed to keep their own values? Sure, we'll uphold the law. We'll expect those in authority to do right. But all authorities in our lives are also human. They, too, were made out of dirt. They will sometimes fail us.

Thank God that He remembers us in our utter weakness because "His faithful love endures forever." May I remember His mercy in my relationships with other broken people. May I look for the good, the beautiful, and the precious still to be found in them.

31
Sharpening Your Ax

Odd how reading a passage of Scripture can bring back old memories. This week, I came to Ecclesiastes 10:10 in my daily Bible reading: "Using a dull ax requires great strength, so sharpen the blade. That's the value of wisdom; it helps you succeed."

That Scripture reminded me of a hot July day, years ago in Illinois. I was hoeing around the tomato plants in our garden and making a hard job of it.

I complained to Walt, "I can't believe how stubborn those weeds are."

"Here, honey, let me have your hoe. I need to sharpen it."

Simple solution! The weeds surrendered to my sharpened hoe.

Seventy years after that battle with the weeds, I am confronted with a similar challenge, a challenge of the mind. A dear friend helped me upgrade to Windows 10. That meant a new software program for one of my projects. Ginnie offered me two choices. One program is comparatively simple, similar to what I now use. I should be able to master it fairly easily. It is reliable and efficient, but it has limitations. Another program is much more sophisticated. It has many more useful features, which would be of inestimable help in my work. But my honest friend warned me, it has a much steeper learning curve. If I committed myself to mastering it, it would save me hours of tedious work. But disciplined study has to come first.

What is true in the physical and mental world is also true in the spiritual world. A loving father knows that to build a relationship with his son, he must spend time with him and learn to know his heart. A caring wife knows that the kind of relationship she yearns to have with her husband will take time and thought. A wise employee will work diligently to master his responsibilities so he can please his supervisor. So why is it that we seem to assume we can have a deep and abiding relationship with God our Creator and King without spending time with Him to learn His heart?

Jeremiah 29:11-14 says:

> "For I know the plans I have for you," says the LORD. "They are plans for good and not for disaster, to give you a future and a hope. In those days when you pray, I will listen. If you look for me wholeheartedly, you will find me. I will be found by you," says the LORD. "I will end your captivity and restore your fortunes. I will gather you out of the nations where I sent you and will bring you home again to your own land."

God promises us we can find Him when we seek Him with all our hearts. It will take time and diligence and a surrendered heart. But oh, what joy and what peace He gives when we come to Him, on purpose, to find Him.

32
The Wrong End of the Telescope

The Caribbean nation of Saint Kitts-Nevis wanted to celebrate Columbus' discovery of their tiny island, so they issued a half-penny stamp picturing him on the deck of the Santa Maria searching the horizon with a telescope. Stamp collectors bought the stamp with glee, thinking the artist had Columbus looking through the wrong end of the telescope. That would have made his voyage disastrous—he might have landed in Antarctica or even Timbuktu! Yes, I know that Timbuktu is in the middle of Africa—but you get the idea. The whole world is distorted if you're using the wrong end of the telescope. It turned out that the error on the stamp was not that the artist didn't draw the telescope right; his error was that the telescope itself wasn't even invented until a hundred years after Columbus sailed for the New World!

But the image of looking at life through the wrong end of a telescope came back to my mind recently, as I tried to help a woman in deep distress. She had been admitted to the hospital dangerously ill, and she was there for several weeks before she was well enough to come home. But while she was in the hospital, her father had called the county health department. He reported that her mobile home was horribly infested with rats and needed to be condemned. The health department agreed and condemned her dilapidated, reeking house. She went from the hospital to an assisted-living facility.

She wept in anger. "While I was sick and not able to take care of myself, he betrayed me and got the health department to condemn my home."

"Why did they condemn it?" I asked.

"Oh, it was filthy, and there were dead rats in the walls."

"What do you think was the motivation of your father?"

"Oh, he thought he was protecting me, I guess."

"Did you need protection?"

She nodded painfully. "Yes. I was in bad shape." Then she added hastily, "Actually, the trailer was his, anyway."

"So what do you think was your father's motivation?"

Her eyes filled with tears. "He loves me." She dashed the tears away with a fist. "So I guess you think I ought to phone him and tell him I forgive him for what he did?" (She was still looking at the problem from the wrong end of the telescope.)

I shook my head. "No. I think you ought to phone him and thank him for loving you so much, he rescued you when you didn't know you needed to be rescued."

How often do we look at a problem, a relationship, or an event and interpret it wrongly because we're looking through the wrong end of the telescope? Have we struggled to find the heart to forgive someone when perhaps we really owe them gratitude? King Solomon said, "Wounds from a sincere friend are better than many kisses from an enemy" (Prov. 27:6).

33
Worth Risking a Life?

On a flight across the Pacific to Japan, Walt and I sat by a man who said, with subdued excitement, "I'm going to climb Mount Everest." He was excited because Mount Everest is the highest mountain in the world. His excitement was subdued because he was very aware of the dangers he faced.

Science has advanced, and the technological world has changed; but that won't do away with the dangers. The winds on Mount Everest still blow at two hundred miles an hour. Irresistible avalanches still hurtle down the ascent paths. Hypothermia, frostbite, snow blindness, and lack of oxygen still kill as they always have.

The statistics are grim. It used to be that one out of three would die trying to reach the summit. In recent years, it has dropped to one out of sixteen. Four out of every ten climbers who have actually made it to the peak died on the way back down. In this last year alone, five climbers died. More than two hundred bodies of climbers lie unburied along the ascents because the dangers are too great to risk their recovery.

Why would someone choose to risk a life with those odds for that climb? Because the mountain is there to be conquered? Understandable. God did command Adam to "govern" the earth (Gen. 1:28), so it's probably built into our genes. I felt some of that the first time I soloed in a little Cessna 152 plane.

A scientist might undertake the climb for important geological or medical research. Many —maybe most—of the advances made in medicine were pioneered by people who risked their lives searching for them. That's true of many inventions in industry, transportation, and flight. We have been blessed by the sacrifices of others. A person might climb Everest just so he could brag about it for the rest of his life. He conquered the highest mountain in the world! Not many people can match that claim.

I've been thinking about that since I've lived my allotted three-score years and ten and more. My name will never appear in the Guinness World Records and likely will never be on the front page of our local paper. I've never done anything worthy of fame in my life. I've spent it doing the ordinary things I felt God wanted me to do. But I do have one special, wonderful accomplishment I can brag about.

Jeremiah 9:23-24 explains:

> This is what the Lord says: "Don't let the wise boast in their wisdom, or the powerful boast in their power, or the rich boast in their riches. But those who wish to boast should boast in this alone: that they truly know me and understand that I am the Lord who demonstrates unfailing love and who brings justice and righteousness to the earth, and that I delight in these things. I, the Lord, have spoken!"

I know the Lord Jesus. I know the awesome Creator of Heaven and earth Himself, and I have experienced His lovingkindness and righteousness. I'll settle for that for my bragging rights. And so can you!

34
Which Child Does Mother Love Best?

She came to live with us when she was five years old, this beloved adopted child of ours. All her young life, she'd been tossed from place to place—some of those places unspeakably evil—and she never knew what she'd done to earn such terrible treatment. So when she came to us, she had a hard time believing that she was deeply loved and deeply valued.

I did what loving mothers do: I rocked her, cuddled her, spent hours whispering sweet nothings in her ears, trying to make up for the years of coldness and neglect.

Then one day, I heard her tell her new younger sister, "Mother loves me best of all—more than she loves Daddy, more than she loves you and John. She loves me more than anybody else in the whole world."

Fortunately, her new big brother and her new little sister had no fears about whether Mother loved them with all her heart. But my heart ached for the child who kept wildly looking for proof she was loved.

So which child *does* Mother love best? It's the child who's asking. Mother loves each one of her children best of all. The coming of a new child into the home doesn't mean Mother's love gets chopped into smaller pieces so each can have a bit. Oh no! Her heart just keeps expanding, and her love just grows deeper with the coming of each new treasured child.

But what about the rebellious kid who kicks at every word, who is unloving and feels unloved? Can a mother really love that kind of child? Absolutely! In fact, he stays especially on her heart as she prays for him and seeks ways to bring him back safely into the family fold.

Do I love each child in exactly the same way? No. One child gives special pleasure in his quick mind and his quirk of character that makes him find humor in odd situations. Another child gives special delight because of her sweet disposition and the joy she finds in every new thing. Another child grabs my heart because she intuitively understands my own frustrations and heartaches, another because of her eternal curiosity. Every child is unique in personality, in emotions, and in physical abilities. Every child gives the father and mother in this home deep pleasure with his unique qualities.

And that's exactly the way your Heavenly Father loves you, except He loves you more deeply, more purely, with even greater pleasure and satisfaction in who you are than any human mother could. When you trusted the Lord Jesus to forgive you for your sins and take you to Heaven, you became a child of God. You are infinitely, eternally loved by Him. He thinks about *you* all the time. You have a unique relationship with Him which no one else on earth can share.

In Psalm 139:16-18 King David said to God, "You saw me before I was born. Every day of my life was recorded in your book. Every moment was laid out before a single day had passed. How precious are your thoughts about me, O God. They cannot be numbered! I can't even count them; they outnumber the grains of sand! And when I wake up, you are still with me!"

I know it's astounding—but true. God thinks about you all day long, every day. Sure, He feels the same way about every one of His creatures. But you are unique. He loves you best of all for what you truly are. It gives Him great pleasure to give you all the treasures of Heaven. In Luke 12:32, Jesus said, "'So don't be afraid, little flock. For it gives your Father great happiness to give you the Kingdom.'" Yes, sweet child, I love you with all My heart. I love you best of all.

35
When You Face a Crisis

When you file a flight plan with the FAA for an instrument take-off, the controller asks, "How many souls on board?" *Souls*—not passengers, not tickets, but real, live, breathing human beings. That must weigh heavily on the minds of pilots when they are suddenly faced with a life-threatening crisis during a flight.

One of our foster children grew up to be a 747 captain for Northwest Airlines. My conversations with Bill always left my heart pounding because he would tell me of the stringent training he underwent in the simulator for responding to emergencies. The simulators were programmed to introduce multiple problems, one after another—things you'd think never could happen on a routine flight. But the intensive, grinding training was essential if a pilot was to be truly prepared for any emergency.

I was reminded of that last week when the news focused on the anniversary of the U.S. Air flight out of LaGuardia that hit a flock of Canada geese and lost all power. The pilot, Captain Chesley Sullenberger, realized he could not make it back to LaGuardia and told air controllers he was going to ditch the plane in the Hudson River. He carefully chose a place near operating boats to maximize their chance of being rescued. Ultimately, all 155 passengers and the crew of five were brought to safety. Captain Sullenberger was the last to leave the airplane, after walking its entire length twice to make sure no one was left behind.

Air traffic controllers said that throughout the transmissions, the captain's voice was quiet and clear. One controller said he actually wept while the plane was going down, but he could not hear a tremor in the voice of the man intent on saving the lives of the people entrusted to his care that day. The crew's award read, "This emergency ditching and evacuation, with the loss of no lives, is a heroic and unique aviation achievement." Newspeople called it the "Miracle on the Hudson."[5]

I have no doubt that God Himself intervened in that flight, no doubt that the courage and commitment of the crew were integral to its safe ending. But when you hear that Captain Sullenberger had logged nearly twenty thousand flight hours and that he is a certified safety expert and a glider pilot, you realize he had the knowledge and the training that helped him save lives that day.

Recently, I read that drill sergeants and coaches like to say, "You don't rise to the occasion, you sink to the level of your training." How does that truth affect you and me? There is no doubt we will face catastrophic emergencies in our lives. How we respond to them depends on how well we have disciplined ourselves day by day in the choices we make. We are in training every day. The level to which we submit ourselves to God's discipline will determine how well we respond when we face a soul-searing crisis.

Hebrews 12:10-11 says, "For our earthly fathers disciplined us for a few years, doing the best they knew how. But God's discipline is always good for us, so that we might share in his holiness. No discipline is enjoyable while it is happening—it's painful! But afterward there will be a peaceful harvest of right living for those who are trained in this way."

I'm in training! I want to be so well-trained that when the emergency comes, I'll be able to handle it rightly. Don't you?

---

5   Amy Tikkanen, "US Airways flight 1549," in *Britannica*, accessed July 18, 2024, https://www.britannica.com/science/disaster.

36
How Can I Do God's Work?

My mother probably never heard of Hannah More; but she was remarkably like that Victorian woman who fought slavery and encouraged young women to use their lives for God in the eighteenth century. Mother would have agreed wholeheartedly when Hannah said, "Idleness among children, as among men, is the root of all evil, and leads to no other evil more certain than ill temper."[6]

Mother did give my five sisters and me time to read good books and play baseball on the vacant lot next door, have tea parties, or put on melodramas on the front porch for the neighborhood children. But she also expected us to help with the housework, make excellent grades in school, practice the piano (or whichever instrument we were learning at the time), work in Daddy's office, teach a Sunday school class, or go with her to help a family in need. She probably did feel that "idleness among children is the root of all evil"!

With that kind of training and inheritance, it's no wonder that to this day, I feel guilty if I haven't accomplished a visible amount of work every day. But that has its problems at this time in my life because I have fewer visible opportunities to serve God. I have trouble reconciling my apparently unproductive life with the Scriptural injunction of "make the most of every opportunity" (Eph. 5:16).

You may feel the same way. Almost any job (and perhaps every job) has some apparently unproductive requirements—boring but necessary things

---

6   Hannah More, *The Works of Hannah More* (New York: Harper & Brothers, 1855), https://archive.org/details/worksofhannahmor00moe/page/n11/mode/2up.

that must be done over and over again. How can you fit all that together and feel like you are doing the work of God?

I cannot describe the comfort I found in Jesus' answer to this problem of mine in John 6. People following Jesus asked Him, "'We want to perform God's works, too. What should we do?'" (John 6:28).

If I had answered their question, I would have said, "Read your Bible. Pray a lot. Talk about Jesus with people who don't know Him. Work hard. Be faithful at church. Be honest. Train your children well." The simple answer I would say is "work! Work hard!"

But none of that is even hinted at in the answer Jesus gave these people. "Jesus told them, 'This is the only work God wants from you: Believe in the one he has sent'" (John 6:29).

How are we to do the work of God? The simple answer (Jesus said) is to believe! Just believe! When you believe in Jesus, you are doing the work of God. He is the One Who decides what He wants you to do today. And it might not be something you could write down on a list of "things accomplished today." Just trust Him. It will be valuable, even if you only believe in Him, because that is all He asks of you!

37
She Didn't Appreciate All He Did for Her

He's a young man, probably in his early thirties. He works steadily at a decent, medium-paying job. His mother is widowed and works at an entry-level job with few benefits. He is concerned for her welfare. He often pays her bills. When her automobile needs repairs, he takes care of it. He is trying to give her security by buying her a house when, and if, he can find one that satisfies her standards.

How does she respond? She always has an objection of some kind. Nothing he does is ever quite good enough. Sure, she's glad he cares about her, but why doesn't he do more? Can't he see she needs something else? Why doesn't he do that, too? It breaks his heart because he's doing everything within his power to give her security and make her happy. He asked me what I thought he could do better.

I could tell her that she ought to thank God for the wonderful son He has given her. Not every mother receives that kind of loving concern from a child. I might give her a little lecture—I'm pretty good at lecturing—about being grateful for what God has given her. I could quote 1 Thessalonians 5:18 to her: "Be thankful in all circumstances, for this is God's will for you who belong to Christ Jesus." But then she hasn't asked for my advice.

So what can I tell him that would ease his load of feeling that he doesn't do enough? What would comfort him for all the unappreciated sacrifices he has made? A good place to start might be Ephesians 6:6-8: "Try to please them all the time, not just when they are watching you. As slaves of Christ, do the will of God with all your heart. Work with enthusiasm, as though you were working for the Lord rather than for people. Remember that the Lord will reward each one of us for the good we do, whether we are slaves or free."I said to him, "Son, whether your mother appreciates it or not, I promise you that the Lord Jesus has seen every kind thing you've done for her. He is pleased with you, even if she isn't. And He is going to reward you for all you've done. So keep doing right because you love the Lord Jesus and because He loves you."

This Scripture may be what God wants you to hear today, too. You may be working sincerely and at personal cost at something the one you're serving doesn't value. It may be a family member, a neighbor, a friend, someone at church, or perhaps a fellow worker. Should you just quit trying? Yes, perhaps, if you are actually hurting them by enabling them to continue in selfish ungratefulness—but not if God Himself laid the burden on you.

Why not change your focus? As the Scripture above says, "Work . . . as though you were working for the Lord, rather than for people." God sees what you are doing. He knows your heart. He senses your sincere motivation. So do it for Him. I promise you, He will reward your faithfulness. So, yes, keep on doing right, whether it is appreciated or not. Do it for Jesus' sake!

38
Come Just as You Are

We once got an invitation to a "Come as You Are" party. The idea was that you weren't to dress up for the party; you had to wear whatever you were wearing when you opened the invitation. I think probably we all cheated a bit—at least, no one came in pajamas!

The Bible tells us that God is planning a wonderful celebration, and it's a "Come as You Are" party. So often, when we are talking to one of our patients about the invitation God has given us to come to His party, someone will say, "I'm going to do it just as soon as I get my life straightened out." Or they might say, "God wouldn't want the likes of me."

But God's invitation isn't "Clean yourself up, and then come to Me." God's invitation is "Come just as you are." The truth is, none of us can get ourselves clean enough to meet a holy God. That's why Jesus died on the cross, so He could pay for every rotten thing we've ever done and give us His righteousness. Ephesians 2:4-5 says, "But God is so rich in mercy, and he loved us so much, that even though we were dead because of our sins, he gave us life when he raised Christ from the dead. (It is only by God's grace that you have been saved!)."

What a party it will be when we get to spend all of eternity enjoying God's wonderful gifts! The next two verses in Ephesians 2 describe it this way: "For he raised us from the dead along with Christ and seated us with him in the heavenly realms because we are united with Christ Jesus. So God can point to us in all future ages as examples of the incredible wealth of his grace and kindness toward us, as shown in all he has done for us who are united with Christ Jesus."

Have you been waiting to get your act together before coming to God? Can you hear Him saying, so tenderly, "Don't wait. Come to Me just as you are. Let me do the 'fixing up' for you"?

39
When A Door Slams Shut

Sometimes in life, it seems as if a door of wonderful opportunity has been slammed shut in your face. It seemed so ideal, so right, you can't help but wonder why God let it happen.

Our daughter and her husband experienced this. They lived in Houston, where he had a lucrative job selling office equipment. True, he often wished he could be in Christian service, rather than spending day after day having to focus on making sales. But they were reconciled to doing what it seemed God had given them. They found the house of their dreams, just exactly what they needed for the family, close to work and church, and at a fair price they could afford. They made an offer, and the owner accepted it immediately.

Imagine their shock when the bank told them their credit was bad, and they could not finance the house. They'd never missed paying a bill on time in their whole life! It turned out that when they bought some appliances two years before, the company had never recorded their very first payment. Every single payment they made in that time had been marked one month late. Fortunately, they had the original receipts and could prove the credit report was wrong, but it killed the contract on the house—a door slammed shut.

But within the month, the Houston economy was hit by a terrible slump. Scores of businesses closed. The real estate market collapsed. In that difficult time, our son-in-law was offered a job in another town, where he could use his gifts to serve God. If the deal on the house had gone through, they couldn't have sold it at the price they paid; they couldn't have taken the job so ideally suited to their gifts. And they learned the wonderful truth that Jesus taught in Revelation 3:7: "'This is the message from the one who is holy and true, the one who has the key of David. What he opens, no one can close; and what he closes, no one can open."

No one can slam shut a door held open by God! As Psalm 37:23 says, "The LORD directs the steps of the godly. He delights in every detail of their lives." God holds the keys to every part of our lives. We need never fear when a door slams shut. It means God is working!

40
Small, Incremental Gains Matter

Baseball has never been one of my favorite sports. It probably goes back to my childhood, playing baseball with the neighbor kids on the vacant lot next door. My sisters assured me that I might manage to hit the ball once in a while if I would just quit squeezing my eyes shut as I swung the bat.

Nevertheless, George Will used a basic baseball principle to make an important observation in one of his political columns in *The Washington Post*. "In baseball, a game without a clock," he writes, "each player on a team that is behind by a bunch of runs is advised to 'stay within yourself.' That baseball lingo means: Do not try to do too much. Small, incremental gains matter because the game goes on until someone makes the 27th out. Until then, there is hope."[7]

I like that. My instinct—and also, perhaps, my training—is to aim for a grand slam, whatever it is I am working on. I want to wow people, but it's also fair to say that I feel a responsibility to do my best for the sake of the company. But many times, that really is not feasible. I may not have the skills, the opportunity, the training, or the wisdom to accomplish something really startling. So wouldn't it be better to make a small, incremental gain that would contribute to the success of the whole operation?

The Scriptures tell us about a woman who did just that. Her story is told in three of the Gospels. Mary of Bethany had sat at the feet of Jesus when He

---

7   George Will, "Can Romney turn this contest around?," *The Washington Post* (Washington, D.C.), October 1, 2012, https://www.washingtonpost.com/opinions/george-will-romney-running-out-of-clock/2012/10/01/55922ea4-0bec-11e2-bb5e-492c0d30bff6_story.html.

came to her home, and she understood that Jesus was going to die for the sins of the world. So in the week He would die, she brought an alabaster bottle of pure perfume to anoint Jesus with to express her love and grief.

It was expensive stuff, and the disciples were caustic in their criticism of her. "Why," said Judas—hypocritically, it turns out, because he was a thief, despite being the treasurer of the group—"we could have fed hundreds of poor people with the money you've wasted here."

"She has done what she could and has anointed my body for burial ahead of time" (Mark 14:8).

She made small, incremental gains. No records were broken, no headlines proclaiming her goodness, no trumpets blown. But she was faithful at what she felt God wanted her to do.

41
How Important Are the Little Things?

S he was a soft-spoken Nebraska farm girl when she came to work as a clerk at the publishing company where I worked years ago. She said she was not accustomed to "city" ways, so she seemed to drift through the day's work at her desk. She sometimes combed her hair and put on make-up after she arrived at work because she didn't hear the alarm clock or her alarm clock didn't go off. She showed equal indifference to the quality of her work in the subscription department.

"Nobody's perfect," she'd explain. "My boss just likes to fuss at me."

I knew her job was at risk, so I tried to befriend her. "Lorraine,[8] what do you really want to do with your life?"

"Be a famous opera singer or artist," she said serenely. "I haven't made up my mind which yet."

"How are you preparing for that?" I asked.

She looked at me in surprise. "They hold me down here. They don't care about anything I want to do," she replied. "All they care about is this old job."

You won't be surprised when I tell you she never became a famous opera singer. She never became an acclaimed artist. She spent her life in mediocrity. The answer to her being unsuccessful might be found in Luke 16:10-12: "'If you are faithful in little things, you will be faithful in large ones. But if you are dishonest in little things, you won't be honest with greater responsibilities. And if you are untrustworthy about worldly wealth, who will trust you with

---

8   Name changed to protect privacy.

the true riches of heaven? And if you are not faithful with other people's things, why should you be trusted with things of your own?'"

Of course, you and I want to do something great with our lives. God wants us to dream, to have holy ambitions. But the first step in doing something great for God is to be faithful in the small matters He has already entrusted to us. Unless we are faithful in the simple things we are already obligated to do, God can't trust us to be faithful with important tasks.

But come to think of it, God has already entrusted us with the true riches of Heaven. How I live my life today can affect others for eternity. Because I talk about Jesus, people expect to see Jesus in me. If they don't see Jesus reflected in my life, I have betrayed the sacred trust given to me by God when He brought me into His family. That must mean there are no truly little tasks. Whatever God gives me to do today is important, no matter how insignificant it may seem to others. May He find me truly faithful!

42
A Confirmed, Guaranteed Reservation

"We're the Handfords. We have a reservation with you for tonight," Walt said to the clerk.

Many years ago, we were in the lobby of a small inn in a small village overlooking Bodega Bay on the Northern California coast. It was a desolate area, and this was the only motel for miles.

The clerk peered at us over her glasses. "I'm sorry. Your room is not available."

"Here's the confirmation number for our reservation for tonight," Walt said firmly.

She looked at the paper as if she'd never seen anything like it. "Yes, sir, I know you have a confirmed reservation, but your room is not available."

We had really looked forward to this brief trip. Walt had spoken all week in San Francisco at a Bible conference. He was exhausted. Now we had a couple of days off before flying back home. We'd rented a car to make the drive to Bodega Bay. Walt's relatives had always told him this place was a "must."

It wasn't the ideal time of year to be in Northern California. It was chilly and foggy. But we'd had a wonderful trip so far. We'd stopped at Muir Woods, one of the few remaining stands of old redwood trees. We were drawn to worship God in its quietness and grandeur. We had thought we'd tour the Point Reyes Lighthouse but were intimidated by the eight hundred or so steps to get down to sea level and back up again, so opted out of that climb.

Now it was dusk, and we were ready for a warm bowl of soup and bed. But we had no room.

The clerk hesitated. "But if you wouldn't mind a different room at the same price—"

"We'll take it," Walt said quickly.

It turned out the "different room" was their luxury suite: two rooms with a kitchenette, a real fireplace with a real log burning, a huge and comfortable bed, the biggest TV screen I'd ever seen, and a big window overlooking Bodega Bay framing an incredible sunset.

God's Word tells us we can have a confirmed, guaranteed reservation for Heaven; but He Himself is the One Who guarantees it, and He is the One who always keeps His Word. (No casual rejection by a hotel clerk here!) Here's the reservation:

> All praise to God, the Father of our Lord Jesus Christ. It is by his great mercy that we have been born again, because God raised Jesus Christ from the dead. Now we live with great expectation, and we have a priceless inheritance—an inheritance that is kept in heaven for you, pure and undefiled, beyond the reach of change and decay. And through your faith, God is protecting you by his power until you receive this salvation, which is ready to be revealed on the last day for all to see.(I Peter 1:3-5).

Here's the confirmed guarantee:

> God also bound himself with an oath, so that those who received the promise could be perfectly sure that he would never change his mind. So God has given both his promise and his oath. These two things are unchangeable because it is impossible for God to lie. Therefore, we who have fled to him for refuge can have great confidence as we hold to the hope that lies before us (Heb. 6:17-18).

When doubts come to mind, like "Am I safe? Is it true? Can I be sure?" remember that God keeps His promises. If you asked Him for eternal life because Christ died in your place for your sins, He gave you a confirmed, guaranteed reservation for Heaven. And the accommodations will be infinitely superior to anything we can possibly imagine!

43
Go With the Strength You Have

You've been there, and so have I—a place where you feel you can't take another step. Your energy is gone, your emotions exhausted, the outcome bleak. There's no time to ask yourself, "How did I get myself into this?" Because the obligation is there, you must meet it.

That was my mood this morning. The list of things I had to do was long; I felt my ability to accomplish them was zilch. The weight of my years pressed me down. I had exhausted my the end of my rope. But as I sat and stewed about my unfulfilled obligations, I remembered something I had just read in the Bible about Gideon.

The Israelites were starving because the Midianites kept stealing everything. Gideon was a hard worker and a faithful worshiper of God. God had chosen him to rescue His people from the enemy. But when God told him this, Gideon answered, "'But Lord . . . how can I rescue Israel? My clan is the weakest in the whole tribe of Manasseh, and I am the least in my entire family!'" (Judges 6:15).

But God was undeterred by Gideon's weaknesses or excuses. He simply answered, "'I will be with you. And you will destroy the Midianites as if you were fighting against one man'" (Judges 6:16).

You may remember the rest of the story. Gideon's small band of three hundred men conquered the immense army of Midian with only clay pots, trumpets, and torches. Gideon obeyed, and it turned out to be God's unconquerable strength was enough to rid the Israelites of their lifelong enemies.

God promises that in His faithfulness, He will enable me to accomplish His will for me today. Maybe you need this reminder as you face a difficult task today. Go with the strength you have and expect your good Heavenly Father to supply His inexhaustible strength in your weakness.

44
My Dad Put His World on Hold

Years ago, I spent several days with my aging father and mother in Tennessee on their little farm.

At breakfast, Daddy said, "Libby, come, take a ride with me. One of the cows didn't come to the barn last night. I'm afraid she's dropped her calf and is in trouble."

My father carried many heavy responsibilities: editing a Christian newspaper that went into 250,000 homes every week, a daily radio broadcast, a publishing company with more than sixty employees, and a demanding evangelistic preaching schedule. But the night before, one of his cows hadn't come to the barn; and he was deeply worried about her welfare. So he put his demanding world on hold while he went to find her.

He saddled his horse, MacArthur, and saddled Jill for me. We rode through several pastures before we found the heifer, lying on her side in a little hollow, a small, wobbly calf leaning on her side.

"She'll die if we don't get her to the barn, get her on her feet, and give her water," Daddy said anxiously.

We rode back to the barn, where he pulled out a canvas sheet attached to a board. He'd learned how to make a "drag sled" growing up on a ranch in west Texas. I remembered I'd seen pictures of Native Americans using something like that.

\When we got back to the cow, Daddy gently rolled the mother cow onto the canvas, tied the board with ropes to MacArthur's saddle, mounted him, and then gently set the horse to drag her to the barn. Her calf tottered after us, bawling in distress. Daddy chose a careful path, avoiding rough patches that might hurt the poor animal. Back at the barn, Daddy and Mr. Martin, his friend and helper, got the cow onto her feet with slings; and in just a little while, she was drinking water, her calf contented beside her.

Only then did Daddy drive to his office to resume his burden of grave responsibilities. Proverbs 12:10 reminds us, "The godly care for their animals, but the wicked are always cruel." Because Daddy was a godly man, the need of that poor cow in distress took precedence over all the important duties that required his attention.

That day, I understood better the joy the Lord Jesus felt when He left all the business of running the universe to come to earth to rescue us poor, lost sinners. Jesus said all His pain and suffering would be worthwhile if only He could save us! The parable of the lost sheep in Luke 15:4-6 expresses it well:

> "If a man has a hundred sheep and one of them gets lost, what will he do? Won't he leave the ninety-nine others in the wilderness and go to search for the one that is lost until he finds it? And when he has found it, he will joyfully carry it home on his shoulders. When he arrives, he will call together his friends and neighbors, saying, 'Rejoice with me because I have found my lost sheep.'"

It was such a joy to see that cow rescued from certain death, content and happy with her calf beside her! But I am shamed when I ask myself the question, "How often have I thought what I was doing was so important that I didn't even notice someone who desperately needed Jesus? What in the world was on my 'to do' list that day that was conceivably more important than the welfare of an eternal soul?" There's a simple answer to that question; and with God's help, I want to answer it well.

45
She Did What She Could

The weatherman predicted we'd have two to five inches of snow one Saturday night, and the snow arrived right on schedule. My children helped prepare me for the siege with a pantry full of food, extra bread and milk in the fridge, and dog chow for little Schatzi. I thought the snow looked absolutely beautiful. Everything that was ugly and broken magically turned into mysterious and lovely shapes.

Though the snow was beautiful to me, it meant long and desperate hours of work for a whole lot of people. I wished I could do something to help. But what could I do? I couldn't even shovel a path from my house to the road, let alone seriously lift a burden for someone else. I did phone several people I knew who lived alone to see if they were safe.

But a woman in a nearby community who felt that same burden for her neighbors didn't just worry; she did something about it. Saturday afternoon, she drove up and down her street, scattering cups full of rock salt. She hoped somehow it might keep the street navigable.

Instead of being grateful, another neighbor posted the story on the community mailbox, ridiculing the woman. "How stupid," he ranted, "that she thought she could help with her measly paper cups of salt!" But he was wrong.

The Bible tells us of a woman who did "what she could" in Mark 14:1-9. Mary brought some costly perfume to anoint Jesus. She somehow understood, when most people didn't, that Jesus would die on the cross within a few days.

That dear woman wanted somehow to express her love and grief for the Savior. Some of the disciples made fun of her for "wasting" the perfume.

> But Jesus replied, "Leave her alone. Why criticize her for doing such a good thing to me? You will always have the poor among you, and you can help them whenever you want to. But you will not always have me. She has done what she could and has anointed my body for burial ahead of time. I tell you the truth, wherever the Good News is preached throughout the world, this woman's deed will be remembered and discussed" (Mark 14:6-9).

How wonderful! She did "what she could." The Lord Jesus valued it so much, He said even we would all treasure her sacrifice.

I think the secret is that God loves to help people who know they are weak but who have a burden to do something good for Him. In Isaiah 40:29-31, God says about Himself, "He gives power to the weak and strength to the powerless. Even youths will become weak and tired, and young men will fall in exhaustion. But those who trust in the LORD will find new strength. They will soar high on wings like eagles. They will run and not grow weary. They will walk and not faint." Thank God for people who see a need and do what they can to meet the need. It's certainly more effective than those who sit around doing nothing and criticizing everybody else. I hope you won't listen to the snide remarks of people when you're trying your best to do something good for God. After all, God is going to make what you do effective when you lean on Him for His strength and wisdom. Yes, even if it is something as simple as throwing cups full of rock salt on the road before a storm!

46
A Rude Shock in My Bible Reading

Ever since I was a teenager, encouraged by my father, I have tried to read my Bible through every year. (Walt and I have found an easy way to manage this by using *The One Year Bible* from Tyndale House. Each day, it offers an Old and New Testament passage, a Psalm, and a Proverb in several different translations.)

I can't express what a joy it has been, day by day and year by year, to hear God speak and to know what is on His heart for me. You'd think by now, after all these years, I'd know the Bible pretty well. But this week, I ran into a Scripture in the New Living Translation that really shocked me. King David prays such a revealing prayer in Psalm 119: "Keep me from lying to myself; give me the privilege of knowing your instructions" (v. 29). Why would anyone want to lie to himself? But evidently, we do!

An example from Scripture comes to mind. You remember the story of Abraham and Sarah, how God promised them they would have more descendants than the stars they could count in the sky (Gen. 15:5). But Sarah got impatient when she didn't have a baby for many years. She figured God had forgotten His promise and decided to take things into her own hands. (The story is told in Genesis 16:1-6.)

She said to Abraham, "Since I can't have a baby myself, I'll let my maid be a surrogate mother for me."

The consequences didn't turn out like she wanted. So then she had the nerve to say to Abraham, "You are responsible for this. Kick this woman out." It was her idea but his fault, she said.

Why did she deceive herself? Perhaps she didn't want to take responsibility for consequences of decisions she herself had made. No wonder King David asked God to "keep me from lying to myself."

What is our protection from lying to ourselves? David continues, "Give me the privilege of knowing your instruction." God's Word can keep us from lying to ourselves.

You can't solve a problem until you know what the real problem is. So God must help us to see what His truth is, and that means admitting we're not smart enough by ourselves to see it. The apostle Paul wrote, "Stop deceiving yourselves. If you think you are wise by this world's standards, you need to become a fool to be truly wise" (1 Cor. 3:18).

The apostle John writes, "If we claim we have no sin, we are only fooling ourselves and not living in the truth" (1 John 1:8).

How often have I lied to myself and blamed someone else when I lost my temper, did a poor piece of work, ate more than I needed, harbored a grudge, felt sorry for myself, or spent more money than I should have?

Dear Lord, please keep me from lying to myself. Give me the privilege of knowing Your Word.

That part of the prayer He has already answered. He has given us the privilege of knowing His Word. Now I must listen to His Word, so I won't lie to myself!

47
A Hot Day, A Hot Radiator, and Seven Hot Travelers

It shouldn't have been a big deal. I'd often driven alone with the children the four hundred miles or so to see my parents. Walt always took great care that my vehicle was in good shape, so I wasn't worried about this trip. Walt and our son John couldn't come until after the Sunday services, so they would follow us on Monday.

I say the trip shouldn't have been a big deal, but it was a searing hot day. As I neared Atlanta, I saw the radiator temperature gauge creeping up. I stopped immediately at a service station. The attendant said it just needed water. He waited for the engine to cool and topped it off for me.

Another fifty miles down the road, the gauge went up again. Another stop at a service station, the attendant said the radiator thermostat had been put in wrong; so he inverted it. About thirty miles down the road, another service man said the radiator cap shouldn't have been so tightly screwed on; so he loosened it.

Now near dusk, the automobile overheating again, and still 150 miles from my destination, I was desperate and near tears. I saw a small, isolated gas station in a deep valley near the interstate, pulled off, and told the attendant my problem.

Unlike the other service men I'd sought help from, he listened to my story, asked me questions, and seemed to think through the problem before he spoke. I was reassured. It seemed he sincerely cared and that I was not just an unprofitable problem to be gotten rid of as quickly as possible. I felt he had integrity—he approached the problem with thoughtfulness.

"I think I know what's wrong," he said.

He settled us in a small waiting area while he back-flushed the radiator and checked for leaks.

Whatever he did, it worked. I drove the rest of the way with no trouble.

(And as you mechanics who read this will ask, the answer is yes, the engine head was cracked. During that week of vacation, Walt spent great father/son time with his boys, working as "backyard mechanics," hoisting the old engine from the Buick by a chain hung from a strong tree limb and installing another engine. Thankfully, we made the trip home with no more trouble.)

That incident happened probably forty-five years ago. That small gas station has long been obliterated by a ten-lane interstate highway, but I often remember with deep thankfulness the gas station operator who acted with such kindness. I couldn't have paid him enough for what he did for me that dark night.

Douglas Adams is attributed with saying, "To give real service you must add something which cannot be bought or measured with money, and that is sincerity and integrity."[9] Whatever task it is that we face today, whatever service we may offer, may God help us to do it with real sincerity and integrity. Only then have we done well the job we were hired to do. "Work willingly at whatever you do, as though you were working for the Lord rather than for people. Remember that the Lord will give you an inheritance as your reward, and that the Master you are serving is Christ" (Col. 3:23-24).

---

9   Douglas Adams, "Thoughts on the Business of Life," *Forbes* online, Accessed July 24, 2024, https://www.forbes.com/quotes/2196.

48
What My Passport Told the Customs Officer

Walt and I were coming back from a three-week trip to visit missionaries in Asia. We'd been on a plane all night from Narita, Japan, to Seattle. We staggered off the plane and went to the baggage claim area to get our luggage, hardly able to function with weariness.

We heard a customs officer say to the man standing next to us, "Sir, tell me about the watch you're wearing,"

A little fearfully, we watched the officer take the man into custody. Shortly afterward, agents took two more people out of the baggage claim area. It was unsettling. How could those agents tell, just by looking, who had broken the law?

As we reclaimed our bags, I remembered that I had left my laptop on board the plane. I hurried back to the gate. The plane we'd flown on was still at the ramp.

I said breathlessly to the agent at the counter, "I left my laptop on that plane. Has it been turned in?" I tried hard not to look as stupid as I felt, and I thought the man could see right through me. I kept babbling about how sorry I was to cause trouble; and I was nervous, wondering how those customs officials could tell, just by looking at people, who had broken the law!

"Let's see your passport," the agent said.

I handed it to him. "I guess you'll know everything about me now," I said, only half-joking.

He swiped the passport on the reader. He looked at the screen, made a shocked face, and gasped, "Oh, oh, what's this?"

"Wha–what? What do you see?"

He said (grimly, I thought), "Your whole life is before me on this screen."

I couldn't imagine what he was seeing. The only traffic ticket I'd ever gotten had been forty years before. What in the world had I done to offend the government of the United States of America?

"What does it say?" I asked, nearly strangled.

His face softened, and he grinned. "Not a thing, except that we have your laptop." And there it was, on the counter by his hand, in plain sight. I would have seen it immediately if I hadn't been so paranoid. "My whole life before him" indeed!

Sometimes, images come to my mind, memories unbidden, of actions I wish I hadn't taken, relationships I hurt, things I have tried to make right and which I have long since confessed to my Heavenly Father. God has forgiven me for them; but sometimes, they still come back to mind as if they were on a customs passport computer, designed to record every mean thought, every thoughtless action I had ever done! I have an enemy who revels in hitting that button, to make me feel worthless and useless. The Bible calls him "the accuser of our brothers and sisters" (Rev. 12:10). Satan loves to see me squirm.

When that happens, I cling to two wonderful Scriptures. Psalm 103:10 says that God " does not punish us for all our sins; he does not deal harshly with us, as we deserve." Why not? Why should I be able to "get by" with sin? I can't. But Jesus traded places with me. He paid the penalty for my sin; and in exchange, He gave me His righteousness. Second Corinthians 5:21 tells us, "For God made Christ, who never sinned, to be the offering for our sin, so that we could be made right with God through Christ."

So when my accuser punches the computer button to pull up my life record, he finds the page absolutely clear, except for a notation at the top, handwritten in red by a nail-scarred hand, "Jesus paid in full."

49
Who Knows Best If the Boy Is Cold?

My son John waved goodbye to me as he left for school one morning. We'd just moved from cold Illinois to sunny South Carolina; but it was still the middle of winter, and the silly child was leaving without a coat.

"Get your jacket on, son. It's cold outside," I called after him.

"Mother," he said reasonably, "I'm ten years old. I ought to know whether I'm cold or not."

He was right. And even if it was colder outside than he realized, he could learn from the experience. He didn't need me hovering over him to make the small, unimportant choices of his life.

I had to learn that lesson all over again when he got his learner's permit. John was a careful driver, but my heart was always in my mouth when he was in the driver's seat.

Walt said to me, "Libby, just let him drive. He needs the experience. You'll be there if he really needs your help. And then you won't worry so much when he's on his own because you'll know he's a good driver."

His father was right. With Walt's wise training and without my hovering, John turned out to be a steady, responsible driver I could trust with my most precious possessions, my children.

It isn't an easy task for a parent to discern how much freedom to give to a child. To micromanage might mean the child would never learn to make wise decisions for himself. To give too much freedom might mean the child would make mistakes not easily reversed. Thank God for His promise: "If you need wisdom, ask our generous God, and he will give it to you. He will not rebuke you for asking" (James 1:5). Parents can find the wisdom from God to know when to hover and when to give freedom.

People in leadership of any kind—whether civic government, church leadership, or business—have to make that same kind of judgment. It isn't an easy task, being a supervisor for example, to know how much latitude to give a new employee and how much supervision he'll need.

Recently, I read online an employee's complaint. "Why do companies hire really smart people and then make them keep stupid rules?"

We'll assume the employee really is smart, like she claims. She wouldn't have been hired unless her employer thought her capable. So the question then is, "Are the company rules really stupid, or do they express a company culture that is integral to their mission statement that the employee doesn't yet understand?"

Sometimes, procedures do stay in place long after their usefulness is gone. A wise employee will call them to his boss' attention but probably not call them "stupid"! "Smart" and "wise" are not synonymous. The boss needs us to have discernment and wisdom, not just "smarts." So an employer might hover as needed until we demonstrate our common sense as well as our competence.

Do you need wisdom today in whatever task God has given to you? Remember, then, to "ask our generous God, and he will give it to you. He will not rebuke you for asking" (James 1:5). God wants to give you wisdom—abundant wisdom—and He won't be impatient with you for asking!

50
Sufficient for the Day

One early morning years ago when we lived in a suburb of Chicago, Walt left home to take my father to catch a plane at Midway Airport. It was usually about a two-hour round trip. But it was winter; and the roads might be icy, so there might be traffic delays. I estimated a generous three hours and figured he'd be back home about 10:00 that morning.

At 11:00, he wasn't home. No big deal. Traffic must be bad.

At noon, I wondered whether he had he a flat tire. I was a little anxious but not too worried. You know Chicago traffic.

By 2:00 p.m., I was sure there had been an accident, no doubt. But surely, it wasn't serious. Someone would call if so.

Around 4:00, I began to wonder where he could be. Even if he'd had car trouble, he could walk to a farmhouse and phone me.

At 6:00, I had worked myself up, sure that he'd been in an accident and was so badly hurt, he couldn't call.

By 7:00 that evening, I had convinced myself that I was now a widow, left all alone in this cruel world. The next phone call would tell me he's dead. I couldn't bear it.

At 8:00, he pulled in the driveway. A tractor-trailer had jackknifed on the icy highway on a long hill. Traffic had been blocked both ways. With frustration in his voice, he explained that it took police all afternoon to get it straightened out. He was glad to be home but exhausted.

That night, I reviewed my day of agony. I suddenly realized that if I were going to spend the rest of my life dreading what might happen, I was going to be miserable all the time. I would spoil every wonderful day God had so graciously given Walt and me. Fretting about trouble that might happen tomorrow does not lessen its pain; it only taints the joy of this good day.

And that's when I came to understand what Jesus meant in His Sermon on the Mount. He said, "'So don't worry about tomorrow, for tomorrow will bring its own worries. Today's trouble is enough for today'" (Matt. 6:34).

Jesus reminded us that birds don't worry about food; they know their Heavenly Father will take care of them. And if He cares about little sparrows, how much more will He care for us, His children (Matt. 6:26)?

Come to think of it, the sheep being cared for by the Good Shepherd in Psalm 23 savored every blade of grass in that green pasture, every drink of water from that pool of still water. They didn't worry about "the darkest valley" ahead (v. 4). Their Shepherd knew all about that; He'd take care of them when they got there, just like He did every day!

Just before that Good Shepherd said to not worry about tomorrow, He reminded us, "Your heavenly Father already knows all your needs. Seek the Kingdom of God above all else, and live righteously, and he will give you everything you need" (Matt. 6:32-33).

So today, I will enjoy every precious gift of my Shepherd. I won't (well, I'll certainly try not to!) worry about what might happen tomorrow and so spoil this good day.

51
Good Fences

"Something there is that doesn't love a wall," said Robert Frost. "The gaps I mean . . . at spring mending-time we find them there." As he and his neighbor rebuild the stone wall between their fields, he says again, "Something there is that doesn't love a wall." But his New England neighbor says simply, "Good fences make good neighbors." [10]

We once saw how that worked out with a couple of our neighbors. They'd had a long-standing dispute over exactly where the boundary was between their two lots. When the one neighbor mowed her lawn, she moved the stone over "just to get the grass cut"; but she'd never move it back. So her neighbor would edge it back, a little at a time, until it was where he thought the lot line lay.

One morning, to our pleasant surprise, we saw a survey crew carefully staking out the lot line, with little stakes flying red ribbons. And the next day, a stone mason came and erected a beautiful low stone wall between the two properties. Suddenly, the two property owners were friends again. That's why "'good fences make good neighbors.'"

Children like fences. They need to know where the boundaries of their lives are. They need the security of knowing what is expected of them. But we adults need fences, too. They help us to guard against temptations that could destroy us.

---

10   Robert Frost, "Mending Wall," Poetry Foundation, Accessed May 27, 2024, https://www.poetryfoundation.org/poems/44266/mending-wall.

A man going through a very difficult time in his marriage was determined to be faithful to his wife. He said, "I keep the door of my heart guarded because I know if I opened it, someone would walk through it."

A marriage needs good fences so that no outsider can despoil it. Employees and employers need good fences—a full understanding on both sides of what is expected. A clear job description is part of that "good fence."

Gene Autry sang, "Don't Fence Me In." What he didn't realize is that fences are for our protection to keep danger out, not to hurt us. And fences often need repair because, as Robert Frost said, "Something there is that doesn't love a wall." Let's check the fences in our lives and see if they need mending.

"Don't cheat your neighbor by moving the ancient boundary markers; don't take the land of defenseless orphans. For their Redeemer is strong; he himself will bring their charges against you" (Prov. 23:10-11).

52
I Taste My Words

Ever been in a conversation with a friend, and you said something and knew immediately by the expression on your friend's face that it was the wrong thing to say? You didn't intend to be mean; you were just careless. But it still hurt. Sadly, sometimes we don't even realize we've hurt someone with our thoughtless talk.

A Scottish woman said, "I taste my words ere they pass my teeth!"

Great idea! If I stop to think how my words would "taste" if they were said to me, then I'll be more likely to encourage people and less likely to offend them.

That must be what King David had in mind when he prayed, "May the words of my mouth and the meditation of my heart be pleasing to you, O LORD, my rock and my redeemer" (Psalm 19:14).

There are a couple important ideas to consider. First, what's in my heart will come out in my conversations. And second, if I am careful to guard what I *think* about, then what I *talk* about will be helpful to others. But thinking right is very hard in this topsy-turvy world we live in. I really need the Lord to be my Strength and to help me be what I deeply want to be.

It sounds simple, but it's not that easy. "Take control of what I say, O LORD, and guard my lips. Don't let me drift toward evil or take part in acts of wickedness. Don't let me share in the delicacies of those who do wrong" (Psalm 141: 3-4).

53
My Möbius Strip of Psalm 138:8

A Möbius strip is fascinating. It's simple to make. You take a long, thin strip of paper, make one twist in it, and join the ends together. Then, if you put an ant to walk a straight line on it (as if you could make an ant walk a straight line!) it would walk the whole surface, inside and out, without ever seeming to walk on the inside. How mysterious is that?

I needed a Möbius strip of Psalm 138:8 this week. You'll know why when you read it: "The LORD will work out his plans for my life—for your faithful love, O LORD, endures forever. Don't abandon me, for you made me."

Recently, Walt and I have been walking through a deep and dark valley, a valley in which we can't discern the end. So there is tremendous comfort in this promise of God's that He will fulfill the purpose for which He created me. He is the awesome God Who flung universes into space. He has the power to do things beyond my imagination. So when He tells me He has a plan for me and that He intends to complete His plan for me, I am comforted. How could it be a fearful thing when I remember that His love—His incomprehensible, passionate commitment of love—shapes His purpose for me? How could He plan anything that would hurt me when He has the power and the enduring love to bless me?

But then that niggling fear comes, as it did for King David when he wrote this Psalm. What if—just possibly—He should forget about me? What if He should suddenly give up on me and abandon me? What if I haven't felt His presence?

And that's where the magic of the Möbius strip works so beautifully. It's an unending circle of assurance and absolute rest. God loves me. He has an incredible plan for my usefulness and good. And when I am afraid He might forget me just for a moment, He reminds me again of His love and faithfulness.

54
But Where's the Incentive to Be Good?

A friend of ours grew up in a home where the mother constantly threatened, "God's watching you all the time. If you are bad, He will punish you hard!"

The problem, the little girl well knew, was that she often *was* bad, even when she was trying to be good! For twenty years, our friend lived in fear of a God Who was always watching her, hoping to catch her being bad so He could whack her hard with a big stick.

Then one day, Walt told her the sweet gospel story—that God loved her so much that He Himself had taken on the guilt of her sin, so she could be holy and without blame. Instead of watching her so He could punish her, He was lovingly and patiently guiding her into truth so she could be free forever from her dread of Hell.

Now that she had trusted Christ, He was helping her, day by day, to recognize temptation and giving her the strength to resist it. Jesus was her Friend, her Helper, her Go-between to God. What a relief it was from constant feelings of guilt and despair she'd felt all her life.

On a visit back home to her parents, she shared this wonderful news that sin could be forgiven and forgotten, already paid for by Jesus' death on the cross. Never again would her mother have to dread facing a holy God, if only she would accept Jesus' gift of salvation.

Her mother listened skeptically. "You mean you could be bad anytime you wanted to because it didn't make any difference? You could go to Heaven, no matter how bad you were?"

"No, Mother, it's not like that. See, when you trust Jesus, He gives you a new heart; and He helps you to want to do right. Because my sin cost Jesus so much, I hate it. And because my sin hurts me, I don't want to sin."

"But where's your incentive to be good?" the mother kept asking.

What the poor mother couldn't understand was that with all her threatening her child to be good, it hadn't helped her do right. It had only made her despair.

What should be our incentive to be good? It should not be to earn God's love. We could never be that good. Nor should it be to compensate for sins we've already committed. How many good acts would you have to do to pay for one bad one? What should be our incentive to be good? It should not be to earn Heaven. We'd have to be perfect to earn entrance into God's holy Heaven. If it were possible to do that, then Jesus didn't need to go through all that suffering He endured on the cross.

So what should be our incentive for "being good"? It should be that when we trust Jesus, we become a child of God. When we take His gift of salvation, God gives us a new heart, so we don't want to sin. And when we do sin, we confess it to Him and get it out of the way. What a life-giving relief that is! What a wonderful incentive that is to do right! As 2 Corinthians 5:14-15 tells us, "Either way, Christ's love controls us. Since we believe that Christ died for all, we also believe that we have all died to our old life. He died for everyone so that those who receive his new life will no longer live for themselves. Instead, they will live for Christ, who died and was raised for them."

55
Things Schatzi Doesn't Worry About

Schatzi leads a dog's life, and she thinks it's pretty cool. She's a small, long-haired dachshund, and her name means "darling" in German.

The other night, I was reading in my bedroom chair. She came to my knees and begged so prettily. She had plenty of food and fresh water; she'd just been outside. I got up to see what she wanted; and she promptly jumped up onto my chair, plopped down, and almost smiled, as if to say, "You can sit on the bed to read, my dear. I prefer this easy chair."

Schatzi can do no tricks. She chases no balls. She barks when my neighbors dare get mail from their own mailboxes. So why should I put up with a dog so absolutely useless? Well, she teaches me so eloquently what my Heavenly Father wants me to learn about Him.

Schatzi doesn't worry about food. She prefers human food and will sneak it when she can. (The other day, she snitched a couple of cream-filled doughnuts; and I didn't know it until I found the empty box in her crate!) She takes for granted that her bowl will be full of dog chow any time she goes to it. Schatzi doesn't worry about where to sleep. It may be under the covers at the foot of my bed, or on the easy chair, or in her crate. But there will be shelter.

Schatzi doesn't worry about her beautiful, long-haired red coat, with its gorgeous plumes of gold around her neck, paws, and tail. She grooms herself and endures baths, but she doesn't think they're really necessary.

Schatzi doesn't worry when I leave; she knows I will always come home again. I give her a doggie bone when I leave. She saves it to celebrate when I get home, which she knows I certainly will. Schatzi will save the bone to celebrate my return home. Schatzi never wakes up in the morning wondering what her job is for that day. She already knows. She's to be wherever in the house I am. If I'm cleaning house, she patiently follows me from room to room, sighing a bit, hoping I'll settle down. If I'm at my desk, she's on her pad at my feet. When I'm playing the piano, she's on the chair beside me. If I'm cooking supper, she's alert and expectant. If she hears me move, she opens her eyes, ready to follow me. Her job, her purpose in life, her reason for being is simply to be where I am. And that's what the Lord wants me to learn from Schatzi.

In Matthew 6:25-33, we see that Jesus says:

> "That is why I tell you not to worry about everyday life—whether you have enough food and drink, or enough clothes to wear. Isn't life more than food, and your body more than clothing? Look at the birds. They don't plant or harvest or store food in barns, for your heavenly Father feeds them. And aren't you far more valuable to him than they are? Can all your worries add a single moment to your life? And why worry about your clothing? Look at the lilies of the field and how they grow. They don't work or make their clothing, yet Solomon in all his glory was not dressed as beautifully as they are. And if God cares so wonderfully for wildflowers that are here today and thrown into the fire tomorrow, he will certainly care for you. Why do you have so little faith? So don't worry about these things, saying, 'What will we eat? What will we drink? What will we wear?' These things dominate the thoughts of unbelievers, but your heavenly Father already knows all your needs. Seek the Kingdom of God above all else, and live righteously, and he will give you everything you need."

Carefree Schatzi teaches me that God will give me everything I need. My purpose in life is to seek His face and His righteousness. He'll take care of all the rest. That's what darling Schatzi is teaching me.

56
Don't Listen to the Noise

"Don't listen to the noise," *The Greenville News* headline said, quoting Clemson Football Assistant Coach Brent Venable's speech to the fall 2018 Clemson football team.[11] What's the noise they're not to listen to? In a list of the top one hundred college football players in 2018, *Sports Illustrated* named nine Tiger players.[12] No other college matched that number. Why wouldn't those young men feel really confident when they line up on the field for the kick-off? And how would that "noise" affect their playing? Might they be too comfortable, too enamored by their achievements that they would not play well? Coach Venable warns, "Don't listen to the noise."

Our Head Coach also says, "Don't listen to the noise." The Lord God, our Creator and gracious Savior, is talking to you and me. What's the noise we're not to listen to? Some of the noise comes from the people around us, and not all of it will be uplifting or encouraging. Some people would enjoy seeing us fail. So they tell us, in insidious, sneaky ways, that we aren't capable of doing what God has told us He wants us to do. Some of the noise comes from our loving friends. They want us to succeed, but they discourage us instead of helping us.

We also have an enemy of our souls. He lies to us. Satan tempts us with the glitter of the good life. We need to resolutely turn away from his deceitful noise.

---

11   Scott Keepfer, "Talent-laden Tigers can't 'listen to the noise,' says assistant coach Brent Venables," *The Greenville News* online, June 22, 2018, https://www.greenvilleonline.com/story/sports/college/clemson/2018/06/22/brent-venables-says-clemson-cant-afford-listen-noise/726276002/.

12   Chris Johnson and Eric Single, "SI's Top 100 College Football Players of 2018," *Sports Illustrated* online, June 18, 2018, https://www.si.com/college/2018/06/19/top-100-player-rankings-2018-full-list.

But some of the noise comes from our own heads. We remember past failures. We see our insufficiencies. We're weakened by our doubts, our fears.

What is the only answer to all this noise? When the prophet Elijah ran away from wicked Queen Jezebel, who'd threatened to kill him, he cowered in a cave on Mount Sinai. You may remember the story found in 1 Kings 19. The Bible says that God sent a whirlwind, then an earthquake, and then a fire. But God was not in any of those noisy, frightening events. "And after the fire there was the sound of a gentle whisper," says verse twelve. God spoke to Elijah in "a gentle whisper."

We must tune out the noise the world makes so that we are able to hear God's "gentle whisper." In His love and mercy, He will guide us. He speaks through a parent, a supervisor, or perhaps just His Word, the Bible. But we can know, in spite of all the dizzying noises around us, just exactly what He wants us to do. In Isaiah 30:19-21, we read:

> O people of Zion, who live in Jerusalem, you will weep no more. He will be gracious if you ask for help. He will surely respond to the sound of your cries. Though the Lord gave you adversity for food and suffering for drink, he will still be with you to teach you. You will see your teacher with your own eyes. Your own ears will hear him. Right behind you a voice will say, "This is the way you should go," whether to the right or to the left.

57
Let Me Tell You My Opinion on That

I grew up in a home where opinions were respected, even if you were a child; and unlike most homes of that era, your opinions were respected, even if you were a girl! Our father and mother trained my five sisters and me to listen carefully, to make informed decisions, and then to express our opinions clearly. So it's not surprising, perhaps, that I have been known to walk up to a group of friends engrossed in a conversation after church and say to them flippantly, "What are we talking about? I have an opinion on it!" (And I usually do have an opinion on it, no matter what they are discussing.)

But I am learning that loudly expressing all of my opinions about everything is really not very smart and certainly not helpful to others. I realized this when I read what George Washington said during the Constitutional Convention in 1787. Although Washington was the president of the convention and a revered war veteran, he seldom entered into the vehement arguments those passionate patriots hurled at each other as they shaped the constitution of this new United States of America.

One of Washington's friends said to him privately, "Sir, I know you have strong opinions about all of these things. Why don't you speak out? Why don't you tell us exactly what you think?"

"I want to speak only on matters of supreme importance," Washington replied carefully. "If I speak out on everything, these men won't realize which things are of most importance. I want to be heard when I speak."[13]

---

13   Catherine Drinker Bowen, *The Miracle at Philadelphia: The Story of the Constitutional Convention* (Unknown, 2010).

He was right. It's a Bible truth:

- Ecclesiastes 5:7 says, "Talk is cheap, like daydreams and other useless activities. Fear God instead."
- James 1:19 says, "Understand this, my dear brothers and sisters: You must all be quick to listen, slow to speak, and slow to get angry."
- Proverbs 10:19 says, "Too much talk leads to sin. Be sensible and keep your mouth shut."

So that means, I think, that I shouldn't pontificate on every small decision others make, like who makes the best barbecue, or which is the fastest road into town, or exactly which shoes the president's wife should have worn. Should I, like George Washington, make informed choices about the truly important issues of life? I absolutely have an obligation to others and to God to share that truth. If I don't, I rob them. That's also a biblical truth:

- Proverbs 18:4 says, "Wise words are like deep waters; wisdom flows from the wise like a bubbling brook."
- Isaiah 50:4 says, "The Sovereign LORD has given me his words of wisdom, so that I know how to comfort the weary. Morning by morning he wakens me and opens my understanding to his will."

If I measure my words, I can offer someone in need "words of wisdom"! Someone deeply distressed and tired of life could be heartened if I share God's words of grace and wisdom. Now I just need to figure out when I need to keep my mouth shut and when I need to open it!

58
Washing Dirty Feet

I remember putting my seven little children to bed one evening and noticing that one of them had really smelly feet. Somehow, I had not corralled him properly to get them clean. So I dumped him back in the bathtub, gave special attention to his ten little pink toes, and hustled him back into his pajamas and so to bed. Did I find the task distasteful? No, that child is precious to me, every square inch of him, dirty feet and all.

So why, then, do I find, at times, other chores in my life so distasteful though equally needed? I know they are necessary, but they make me feel as if I'm unimportant, just a cog in the machinery of life. You may sometimes feel the same way. Perhaps all you do all day is to tote up numbers, tag and bag clothes brought in for dry cleaning, clean restrooms, or fry hamburgers. You do it because it's your job, but you'll have to do it over again tomorrow. And likely, no one will even notice! Even in middle and upper management, there are repetitive tasks that can't be delegated and must be done, but they seem to have so little value. It sure isn't the life you envisioned when they handed you your diploma.

They call it a "midlife crisis"; but it can happen anytime, at any task, under any circumstance. And I suspect that millionaires are as susceptible as ditch-diggers.

Years ago, I heard Dr. Bob Jones, Sr. say something like this: "If you know Christ as your Savior, you serve Him as much washing dishes as singing in the choir. Taking out the garbage is as Christian as teaching a Sunday school class. The Christian life is not divided into the secular and the sacred. Everything in life is sacred for a Christian. Every dish is a burning bush. Even the nursery floor is holy ground. Wherever you find yourself, you are God's temple; and you can glorify Him there."

What a comfort that was to me when I was a young and exhausted mother! And how comforting it should be to all of us when the ordinary tasks of life seem unimportant.

The Lord Jesus Himself is our holy Example in this. On the very last night before He was crucified, He took off His robe, tied a towel around His waist, brought a pail of water into the room, and began to wash the dirty, smelly feet of the disciples. It was a filthy task, one usually assigned to the lowest slave in a household, and totally inappropriate for Jesus Christ, Creator of Heaven and earth, the One Who flung the starts into space!

Peter, a disciple, thought it most degrading, and told Him in no uncertain tones not to be absurd! But Jesus answered:

> "You call me 'Teacher' and 'Lord,' and you are right, because that's what I am. And since I, your Lord and Teacher, have washed your feet, you ought to wash each other's feet. I have given you an example to follow. Do as I have done to you. I tell you the truth, slaves are not greater than their master. Nor is the messenger more important than the one who sends the message. Now that you know these things, God will bless you for doing them" (John 13:13-17).

So, whatever the task you must do today, repetitive and boring as it might seem, do it in the name of the Lord Jesus. Jesus was, and is, eternal God; but He gladly washed smelly feet with love and humility. And so can we.

59
Does God Enjoy Seeing Us Squirm?

Last week, a friend told me of an ordeal she was going through. She needed at least twenty people to register for an event she'd planned, or she would owe a great deal of money. She'd been praying very earnestly for help; but the day before we talked, she had only two registrations. But that morning, she told me she had received another twenty, more than enough to pay all the bills.

"I guess God just enjoys seeing us squirm," she said. She didn't sound very grateful for the answer to prayer; she sounded rather unhappy with God because He'd made her wait a whole day for the answer!

You and I have both gone through times when we wondered why God didn't relieve the burden, why He made us wait before He answered our earnest, heartfelt prayers. Was God really up in Heaven enjoying watching us squirm like a worm on a fish hook?

It's a terrible accusation. It ignores the daily, hourly, even minute-by-minute gifts God gives us bountifully and without grudge. Worse, in some sense, it trashes the overwhelming gift Jesus gave to us when He suffered agony on the cross just so He could give us eternal life. So why doesn't God give us immediate relief when we ask for His help? It's not because He enjoys watching us squirm. On the contrary, Lamentations 3:32-33 says, "Though he brings grief, he also shows compassion because of the greatness of his unfailing love. For he does not enjoy hurting people or causing them sorrow." So whatever He does is purposeful and for our eternal good. Because He is infinite God and we are human beings, we might not be able to understand why even if He explained it. But there is wonderful insight given to us in

James 1:2-3: "Dear brothers and sisters, when troubles of any kind come your way, consider it an opportunity for great joy. For you know that when your faith is tested, your endurance has a chance to grow."

What's the take-home value? Sometimes, God does let us wait before answering our prayers. But He does it because He is building strong character in our hearts, so we'll be ready for anything! So what response should I make when trouble comes my way? With God helping me, I'll make it an opportunity for joy!

60
Stop Talking and Find Out the Truth

Those of you born after 1960 have probably never heard of Walter Lippman. He was a prolific journalist and philosopher, adviser to presidents, and founder of the *New Republic* magazine. He was born in a Jewish home in 1889, educated at Harvard, and died in 1974, deeply respected for his integrity and commitment to truth.

One of his major concerns was the influence that journalists and public speakers have on society. He thought that "people, including journalists, are more apt to believe 'the pictures in their heads' than to come to judgment by critical thinking.

"Ordinary citizens can't judge public issues rationally," he thought, "since the speed and condensation required in the mass media tend to produce slogans rather than interpretations." [14]

Yet a cryptoquote I read recently quotes him as saying, "Many a time I have wanted to stop talking and find out what I really believed." [15]

What would Lippman think of the incalculable impact of today's social media, where anyone can post anything about any situation without verifying the facts? It can be sent around the world in minutes, and many who read it will not search for facts but simply take it as truth.

An email may have the same sense of urgency. It seems to be expected that any receiver of an email ought to respond within a few hours, regardless

---

14 *New World Encyclopedia*, s.v. "Walter Lippmann," Accessed July 24, 2024, https://www. newworldencyclopedia.org/entry/Walter_Lippmann.

15 Walter Lippmann, "Walter Lippmann Quote," Libquotes.com, Accessed July 24, 2024, libquotes.com/walter-lippmann/quote/lbg5u0m.

of how important the issue is. But to make a quick decision allows no time for gathering of facts, testing the information, or thinking how it will affect the outcome. The expectation of an immediate answer seems to lessen our ability to handle an email wisely.

Phone texting seems to put even greater pressure on quick answers. But does the one who texts always have the right to an immediate answer? Shouldn't the receiver be given time to think a matter through?

The apostle Paul wrote, "Test everything that is said. Hold on to what is good" (1 Thess. 5:21). The Bible also tells us that the Christians in Berea "were more open-minded than those in Thessalonica, and they listened eagerly to Paul's message. They searched the Scriptures day after day to see if Paul and Silas were teaching the truth" (Acts 17:11).

Since I tend to talk a lot and express my opinions strongly, I may need to "stop talking" and collect the facts before making a stupid statement. Maybe you will find it wise to do so, too!

61
Daddy Bought a Brand-New Dark Red Buick

Back in the 1940s, when I was a teenager, Daddy bought a brand new, dark red Buick. He was a very frugal man, and he seldom made such an expensive purchase. He was a gospel preacher; and he had driven thousands of miles every year in aged, secondhand automobiles. Winter after winter in the freezing Illinois climate, he had struggled to get his ancient vehicles to start and sometimes missed an important speaking engagement because of a breakdown. So my sisters and I all thought the new car a truly beautiful thing, sitting there in the Rice driveway, adding real class to the neighborhood!

One day, I thought of a way I could help my daddy keep that automobile looking beautiful. I got a can of automobile paint cleaner and set about to polish that bright surface. I couldn't see much difference in the result, but I knew my daddy would be so pleased at my thoughtfulness.

I watched his face when he came home and surveyed my work. It didn't reflect the delight I expected to see. He explained to me gently that the kind of automobile paint cleaner I had used should not have been used on that particular surface. I had actually dulled the surface, rather than polishing it. He didn't rebuke me, as he certainly had a right to do. He didn't need to. I was devastated.

The other day, I felt a similar shame when I had tried to do something good for my Heavenly Father. A workman had done some repairs on our home. I was pleased with his work; and as I paid him, I expressed my thanks. Then, because I'm so glad that Jesus died for my sins so I could go to Heaven,

I tried to share the Good News with him. We had an interesting conversation for a while; but then he got agitated, jumped up, and said, "I don't want to talk about it anymore!"

I apologized, asked him to forgive me, and promised I wouldn't talk about it again unless he brought it up. But I was devastated. How could my wanting to please my Heavenly Father turn out so disastrously?

A friend pointed out to me a Scripture I really needed to hear. She reminded me that when King David wanted to build a temple for the Lord, God said, "No. You've been a man of war. Your son Solomon will build it" (see 1 Chron. 28:3). So when Solomon dedicated the temple he'd built, he said, "But the LORD told [my father, David], 'You wanted to build the Temple to honor my name. Your intention is good'" (1 Kings 8:18). My friend reminded me that God knows my heart; and He was pleased that I wanted to do something for Him, even if it didn't work out well.

I am comforted that God knows all about me, my weaknesses, my failures, my longings. King David wrote, "O God, you know how foolish I am; my sins cannot be hidden from you" (Psalm 69:5). But God also knows that I love Him, however imperfectly, and He knows that my deep down heart's desire is to please Him. I am comforted by what King David said in Psalm 103:13-14: "The LORD is like a father to his children, tender and compassionate to those who fear him. For he knows how weak we are; he remembers we are only dust."

So maybe God can use my inept words to do His work in the heart of someone who really needs to hear His Words of forgiveness and grace.

62
A Different Kind of Business Call

I admit it. When I dialed customer service, I was irritated. The phone company had told me they had a free new phone so I could use their new G3 service. But after four trips to the phone store to get it, it was still out of stock. No, they couldn't hold one for me. Just keep coming in.

Then, as an afterthought, the salesperson said, "Call 611 for customer service. They can help you."

I dialed 611. You know the routine: "This call may be monitored . . . Dial one for repairs, two for sales, three for limbo . . . To repeat this message . . . enter your code . . . not a valid number . . . say yes or no . . . to repeat . . ."

In frustration, I punched zero; and to my surprise, a young man answered immediately and cheerfully. Yes, he could help me. We got through the essentials of my business easily enough. Then I told the young man that I needed the account to be put in my name.

"I lost my husband last year," I said, and try as hard as I could, my voice still broke on the words.

There was a long pause. The voice on the phone said, "I lost my son last year, too," and I could hear the tears in his voice.

"I'm so sorry. Did you know that God wept with you? He knows how bad it hurt, and He wants to comfort you. The Bible says, 'In all [our] distress he too [is] distressed.'"[16]

Another long silence followed. I couldn't tell if he was busy working on my account or too brokenhearted to talk.

---

16   Isaiah 63:9, NIV

He ventured, "He'd just been born . . . It was so hard . . . How long were you married?"

"Sixty-seven years"

"Wow! Imagine!"

"Do you and your wife know how much Jesus loves you?"

"I was raised a Catholic. Then Mother started going to the Mormon church, and it was that or work all day. So I went; but really, I'm not anything."

"I'm not talking about church. I'm talking about your knowing that Jesus died on the cross so He could pay for your sins and bring to you Heaven. That's where your baby boy is; and if you trust Jesus to forgive you for your sins, you'll get to see him someday."

Another long silence stretched between us.

"My wife and have been listening to a Christian radio station."

"That's great."

"And we watched that movie *Courageous*. And what they said about Heaven . . . Well, we've started going to church."

"That's a good movie. It's true to the Bible. Be sure to choose a church where the minister tells you what the Bible says."

Another long silence occurred. "After the baby died, we went on a cruise. While we were on it, we found out we were pregnant. Now we have a baby girl, and she's so sweet."

"She was God's special gift to you, wasn't she?"

More silence followed before he tentatively said, "My wife and I—well, we thought maybe some good would come out of this. I was drinking too much and doing bad stuff. Now I know that's not the way I want to live my life."

"Yeah. You need God to help you be the kind of daddy your baby girl needs . . . Say, am I keeping you from getting your work done?"

"No. I'm waiting for my supervisor to okay your order. I really like talking to you."

"Then let me pray with you before you have to go."

Another silence echoed from his side of the phone. Then he said, "Your phone is on its way. And thank you, Mrs. Handford, so much."

What a script of God's grace! Me—impatient and frustrated with store workers but somewhere out there, in a cubicle in a corporate office, a young man with an aching heart needed to hear about the merciful God, Who was patiently blocking phone lines, delaying product shipments, and weaving together the elements so a young stranger and his wife could hear the words of everlasting life. Imagine serving a great God like that!

My new phone arrived two days later.

As Psalm 103:8 says, "The LORD is compassionate and merciful, slow to get angry and filled with unfailing love."

63
My Bewildering Battle with the Second Law of Thermodynamics

If you've raised a teenager, you know all about the second law of thermodynamics whether you realize it or not. At least, that's when I first learned about it. I was trying to teach my kids to keep their rooms clean, but the second law of thermodynamics intervened. I couldn't fight off the chaos. I gave up and asked them just to please keep their bedroom doors shut when company came. Albert Einstein called this law the most basic law of all science. Basically, it says that everything in our universe, when left to itself, tends toward more and more disorder.

It operates in all parts of life. Buy a new automobile? It's going to need repairs. Plant a garden? Weeds will proliferate faster than the tomatoes. Build a house? The roof will eventually leak. It's a law that frets evolutionists because they can't alter it to fit their theories. It's the law that makes environmentalists worry about global warming.

Is that bleak news? No, it's not because it has a qualifying clause: "everything in the universe, *when left to itself,* tends toward more and more disorder." The Creator of our universe does not leave it to itself to degenerate into chaos. He is intimately concerned about caring for the human beings He created with such joy. In Job 38:4-11, God asks:

> "Where were you when I laid the foundations of the earth? Tell me, if you know so much. Who determined its dimensions and stretched out the surveying line? What supports its foundations,

and who laid its cornerstone as the morning stars sang together and all the angels shouted for joy? Who kept the sea inside its boundaries as it burst from the womb, and as I clothed it with clouds and wrapped it in thick darkness? For I locked it behind barred gates, limiting its shores. I said, 'This far and no farther will you come. Here your proud waves must stop!'"

What wonderful news that is! When God created this beautiful world, He committed Himself to guarding it and managing it for the people He loved so dearly. Yes, I absolutely need to do my part to protect the earth's resources, but my best isn't enough to stop the natural tendency to chaos. My Heavenly Father takes that responsibility, and I can rest in His goodness. The world isn't going to end in a whimper because He's watching over it.

Here's the way Colossians 1:16-17 puts it: "For through him God created everything in the heavenly realms and on earth. He made the things we can see and the things we can't see—such as thrones, kingdoms, rulers, and authorities in the unseen world. Everything was created through him and for him. He existed before anything else, and he holds all creation together."

So much for the second law of thermodynamics. Don't expect me to try to explain the first and third laws. You'll have to do that research for yourself. Meanwhile, thank God that He's in control of this universe and watching over you and me in love.

64
The Little Engine That Couldn't

Remember the refrain from the children's book, *The Little Engine That Could*? As the small engine worked to pull an impossible load, it sang, "I think I can! I think I can!"

That engine, built only to shuttle locomotives from place to place, was asked to carry a trainload of toys for children up over a high mountain. I think I remember a clown riding on the coal car and a giraffe's head sticking above the toys. But "the little engine that could" was willing to try. And when he got to the top of the mountain, he merrily sang, "I know I can! I know I can!"[17]

That could have been the John R. Rice family motto. Mother and Daddy were so committed to serving God with all their hearts that they took on enormous projects, mind-defying projects; and by faithful, thoughtful work and God's help, they accomplished wonderful things.

So when Daddy gave us Rice sisters a project to handle, we didn't often venture to say, "Daddy, I don't think I can do that." However reluctantly, we attempted what he wanted; and with God's help and Mother and Daddy's wise example, we did accomplish some things we didn't think we could.

But that was back in the 1930s and '40s. I'm no longer a teenager. Nothing is easy for me to do anymore. I can't see well. I can't hear well. I can't walk well. I don't always remember well. But my lifelong burden to help people know the Lord still lies heavily on me, and that causes conflict in my heart. The

---

17   Watty Piper, *The Little Engine That Could* (New York City: Grosset and Dunlap, 2001).

other morning, I found myself saying to the Lord about a certain obligation, "I don't think I can do it!"

But that morning's Scripture was the story of Gideon. (It is interesting to see how often the scheduled Bible passage is exactly what I'm going to need that day!) The angel of God sat under a tree and said to Gideon, "'Mighty hero, the LORD is with you!'" (Judges 6:12).

God had a mission for Gideon to free Israel from their terrible enemy, the Midianites. But Gideon thought God was making a huge mistake.

Gideon answered, "My clan is the weakest in the whole tribe of Manasseh, and I am the least in my entire family!" (Judges 6:15). But the Lord said to Gideon: "'Go with the strength you have,'" (Judges 6:14). Sure enough, Gideon's "little" strength, enabled by God's mighty strength, was enough to conquer the formidable Midianites with only three hundred men.

Shouldn't I expect the same help from God? Yes, He has made the same promise to me. I must do today whatever God wants of me with what little strength I feel I have. And so must you because He has the power to help us do what needs to be done. As God encourages us in 2 Corinthians 12:9, "'My grace is all you need. My power works best in weakness.'"

God can use us, no matter how inadequate we feel. That's all God expects of us: just do what He told us to do. He will use His strength, wisdom, and love to accomplish His work through us. So today, I'm going to say, "I think I can," and maybe I will be a little engine that could after all!

65
Transformational Leadership

My baby sister is working on her Ph.D. in leadership. Her advising professor, who had followed with great admiration our father's long ministry, suggested she write her dissertation on our father's "transformational leadership."

Daddy would be amused at the terminology. He probably wouldn't have described his leadership as "individualized consideration, intellectual stimulation, inspirational motivation, and idealized influence" like psychologists do. But as my sister Joy has analyzed his lifelong passion as a pastor, a leader of Christian leaders, an influential writer and editor, and most certainly, as a father, she finds he was truly a transformational leader.

As a pastor, he was not content simply to bring people to Christ, to let them settle for an arid rule-keeping rigidity. He followed up on their decisions, taught them joy in a personal relationship with God, established them in their faith, and then passed on to them his passion for reaching others with the gospel.

As a father, he was not content simply to hand down to his six daughters a list of expectations. He let us make decisions, then held us accountable for them. We saw him live his life with love and compassion while teaching us to do right. He ignited in our hearts a yearning to love God and serve Him as he and Mother did. As an employer, he didn't hand down written edicts from his office. He made every employee understand the essential value of his job. His office door was open. He invited suggestions and input and put them into practice when viable. He kept before everyone the vision of what God had call that ministry to do, and now, years later, employees he trained still do their important work.

Why am I telling you all this? As I've thought of it, every one of us has some sort of leadership role. Whatever job we are doing, we are influencing others. So we need to be purposeful, analytical, passionate in every relationship, helping to "transform" others to be all they can be. This is a good biblical principle.

The apostle Paul wrote to his young protégé Timothy, "Timothy, my dear son, be strong through the grace that God gives you in Christ Jesus. You have heard me teach things that have been confirmed by many reliable witnesses. Now teach these truths to other trustworthy people who will be able to pass them on to others" (2 Tim. 2:1-2).

This is true for parents. Psalm 78:5-6 says God "gave his instructions to Israel. He commanded our ancestors to teach them to their children, so the next generation might know them—even the children not yet born—and they in turn will teach their own children." How we lead others is truly critical. If we neglect to influence just one generation, the message might be lost forever to future generations.

66
Stress-Free Living?

The newspaper columnist "Dear Abby" recently published a letter from a man complaining of the stresses in his life and asking, "Don't I have a right to a stress-free life?" He craved the approval of his family about some dubious lifestyle choices he was making, and they wouldn't condone them.

"Yes," answered dear Abby, "of course you have a right to a life without stress. Go ahead and move away from your family and join your friend."[18]

A life without stress? Are you joking? What planet was the poor man living on? And how did Dear Abby think he could avoid the stresses of life by moving to another city? Of course, all of life is fraught with stress. We are human beings, and we face the uncertainties of life every day. We must earn money for food and shelter, find protection from disease and accident, risk political upheaval, love and be loved, interact with unreasonable human beings. If we love someone, we risk their loss. But if we shun relationships, we face loneliness and isolation. How can any human being escape the stresses of life?

As I read that newspaper article, I remembered a night long ago. I was nine years old, sitting alone in the dark on the wooden steps of our front porch in Dallas. As I looked up at the glittering stars of the Milky Way in the Texas night sky, I was overwhelmed by the vastness of God's creation and my fragile humanity. I said to Him that night, "God, you have no idea how hard it is to be nine years old and have so many troubles."

---

18   https://www.uexpress.com/life/dearabby/2024/05/20.

(You may smile at that. After all, I had a father and mother who really did take wonderful care of me, in spite of the burdens they bore. Daddy pastored a huge church congregation and carried them on his heart all the time. In those lean days, he had to provide for the family. Mother struggled in those Depression years to put nutritious food on the table for a large family and many guests. She sewed our clothes, supervised our many activities in music and sports, and taught a big Sunday school class of young women. What were my burdens compared to theirs?)

And I was very wrong in thinking God didn't understand me and my "troubles." Jesus, God Himself, once came to earth to live the life we live so He would understand our worries and have compassion for our bleak condition. He was once a nine-year-old boy with more "troubles" than I've ever known, certainly. He had younger brothers who scoffed at Him. He had the reputation around town that He'd been "born in sin," out of wedlock. He was hated simply because He was so very good.

But Jesus endured every temptation ever known to any human being just so He could help us when we are overwhelmed by the stresses of life. Hebrews 4:15-16 says, "This High Priest of ours understands our weaknesses, for he faced all of the same testings we do, yet he did not sin. So let us come boldly to the throne of our gracious God. There we will receive his mercy, and we will find grace to help us when we need it most."

So even now, many years later, as I struggle with the stresses of old age, I receive His mercy (oh, the grace of it!) and find Him always helping me when I need Him, just as He did for that nine-year-old child so long ago.

67
Best Candidate for the Job

The first morning after we got to London, we boarded one of those trademark double-decker red buses to go to the Tower of London. It's the famous fortress where people like Sir Walter Raleigh and Lady Jane Gray were beheaded. It's also the place where the priceless Crown Jewels are kept in a huge windowless bank vault. The biggest white diamond in the world is mounted in the scepter of King Edward VII. It's the Cullinan diamond, and it weighs—hold your breath—530.2 carats! It's no wonder they hire strong, husky "Beefeaters," men seasoned with years of experience and training, to guard the place.

That cold, rainy Wednesday morning, the line at the entrance was short; and because it was not crowded, we were permitted to stay in the jewel room as long as we liked. One of the Beefeaters who explained the jewels to us was, to our surprise, a woman! We'd never seen that before. And when we got home, a line in *Time* magazine explained it.

"'She was the best candidate for the job,' [said] Natasha Woollard, spokeswoman for the Tower of London, about appointing a woman as one of the tower's guardians—nicknamed Beefeaters—for the first time in the 522-year history of the job.'"[19]

We said this story involves you, and it does because you are the very best candidate for the job you fill so beautifully. That's true not only about your work. You are the very best candidate for your job as a husband or a wife. You

---

19 "Verbatim: Jan. 22, 2007," *Time*, January 11, 2007, https://time.com/archive/6679616/verbatim-jan-22-2007.

are the very best candidate for your job as a parent. (Yes, the kids sometimes make you feel like you are incompetent, but they are wrong.) You are the best candidate for your job as a civic volunteer or as a church member.

Listen to what God says in Philippians 2:12-13: "Work hard to show the results of your salvation, obeying God with deep reverence and fear. For God is working in you, giving you the desire and the power to do what pleases him."

When you honor God in your life, He gives you the wisdom and energy to do what He wants you to do. And what a delight it is to know you can do exactly what God wants you to do because He's promised to help you!

68
Mayfield's Banana Split Ice Cream

A friend of ours works with a ministry for women in recovery from drugs, liquor, or theft. In this home, they get real, lasting help as they come to know Christ and His enduring help in their temptations. But often, they are there by court order; and though they are glad not to be in prison, they still find it hard to be away from home and family.

One young woman was finding it especially difficult. "You know the first thing I'm gonna do when I get out of here?" she asked. "I'm gonna buy me a whole half gallon of Mayfield banana split ice cream."

The girls all laughed sympathetically. Each of them had some memory of home that they longed to experience again, just as she did.

The next morning, a woman, a friend of the ministry, walked hesitantly into the reception area of the home. "I feel really stupid about this," she explained. "I don't understand this at all." She held out a plastic grocery bag. "I know you are going to think it's silly, too, but I think the Lord told me to do this . . . Anyhow," she said desperately, "I felt like God told me to buy this Mayfield banana split ice cream and bring it here. I bought enough for all of you."

She flushed when the group of young women standing nearby burst into laughter. She was already feeling diffident about her errand, and their response really embarrassed her.

"Mayfield's!" one gasped.

"Banana split ice cream!" squealed the one who had originally mentioned it to the group.

"It's yours," another said. "God sent it to you!"

The girl who had wished for the ice cream turned with gratitude to the woman. "Thank you, thank you. If God cares this much about me, then I think I can make it!"

Can you imagine what that gift of ice cream did for the young woman struggling with temptation? She learned her Heavenly Father was intimately concerned with her needs and her longings. His unexpected gift gave her tangible hope for the future. But imagine, too, the joy of the woman who followed the prompting of the Holy Spirit in her heart, even when it seemed absolute foolishness to her. She was truly an instrument of God's grace. Remember the words of Psalm 145:8-9: "The LORD is merciful and compassionate, slow to get angry and filled with unfailing love. The LORD is good to everyone. He showers compassion on all his creation."

69
Who Is It I Am Really Trusting?

For fifteen years, though I didn't realize it, I put my trust in the Equitable Life Assurance Company of the United States of America to take care of me and my family. You understand, I would have told you that, of course, I trusted God to take care of us. But if some disaster should befall my beloved Walt, at least I'd have a home clear of debt because of Equitable.

When Walt accepted a pastorate in Greenville, South Carolina, we came to live in a lovely church parsonage. Suddenly, I realized that if I lost Walt, I would have no home for my seven children and no income. I had no Equitable Life Assurance. And that was when I realized how strong my faith had been in Equitable!

I heard my Heavenly Father say very quietly, "Libby, I have been here all the time, watching over you and protecting you and the family all these years. Equitable Life Assurance can't assure you of anything, not even life itself, in spite of its name! I promise I will keep on taking care of all of you for the rest of your lives."

God has kept every promise He made to me in the fifty-six years since that day. I have been a slow learner; but I am learning to trust Him, and Him alone, rather than any institution, or investment, or Medicare, or church family, or even my dear children—

Except that I nearly had a meltdown last week, when a feeling of utter insufficiency hit me. I looked at my schedule for the week and thought, *I'm too old for all of this. I don't have the strength, the emotions, the presence of mind to handle all these demands. I must have been out of my mind to agree to them. What in the world was I thinking?*

And the Lord said to me, so quietly (and still so patiently), "Libby, you don't have to do all of those things today. All you have to do is meet today's schedule. I have promised you strength and wisdom for today. Why are you worrying about tomorrow? That won't help you do what I have in mind for you today." He kept His promise. He helped me do what I had to do.

That is exactly what Jesus promised in Matthew 6:25-30:

> "That is why I tell you not to worry about everyday life—whether you have enough food and drink, or enough clothes to wear. Isn't life more than food, and your body more than clothing? Look at the birds. They don't plant or harvest or store food in barns, for your heavenly Father feeds them. And aren't you far more valuable to him than they are? Can all your worries add a single moment to your life? And why worry about your clothing? Look at the lilies of the field and how they grow. They don't work or make their clothing, yet Solomon in all his glory was not dressed as beautifully as they are. And if God cares so wonderfully for wildflowers that are here today and thrown into the fire tomorrow, he will certainly care for you. Why do you have so little faith?"

This reminder and promise are from God. If you make God's will your primary concern, you will find He will meet your needs today, and tomorrow, and forever.

70
Stars in My Eyes

Oh, I've had stars in my eyes lots of times . . .

. . . like the cool October night when Walt and I stood under the elm trees, and he told me he loved me and asked me to marry him.

. . . like the hot afternoon I landed the Cessna 150 airplane at the Greenville Downtown Airport, and the FAA examiner handed me my new pilot's license.

. . . like the balmy evening the adoption agency social worker put a tiny bundle wrapped in a pale yellow blanket into our arms, and we looked on our baby son's dear face for the first time.

But stars in your eyes can sometimes blind you to reality. Driving home in the evenings, I began to notice that the headlights of approaching automobiles seemed to increasingly shatter into stars. Now those were stars I didn't want to see! My doctor had warned me that sometime in the future, I could expect to have cataracts; so I knew what to do. I made an appointment to see my doctor.

While I waited for surgery, I realized what a terrible handicap it was not to be able to see well. The bright colors of spring faded into grays. Reading a newspaper in ten-point type became a chore. Street signs were difficult to read. Pictures of the sweet faces of my grandchildren blurred. The only answer was surgery; and until I had it, life would be frustrating.

If I had denied that I had a handicap and had continued to drive at night, I would have been a threat to everyone I met. If I had put off having surgery, my sight would have kept deteriorating. Admitting I was seeing stars instead of headlights was my first step to good eyesight and safety.

But why would anyone *not* admit their blindness and their need for intervention? Strangely, this can happen when we are trapped in spiritual darkness and confronted by the truth. We may not *want* to see the truth; and as Jesus said, "'Wherever your treasure is, there the desires of your heart will also be. Your eye is like a lamp that provides light for your body. When your eye is healthy, your whole body is filled with light. But when your eye is unhealthy, your whole body is filled with darkness. And if the light you think you have is actually darkness, how deep that darkness is!'" (Matt. 6:21-23).

Yes, I want to walk in the light and "let sunshine in my soul." To do that, I must be aware of my flawed thinking and realize I might be rejecting a truth God wants me to acknowledge. It's only as I listen to His Word and examine my heart that I will be able to know if I have shut out the light and that I'm walking in darkness.

71

When You Find Yourself Feeling Inadequate

Do you ever feel inadequate to do something someone expects of you? I don't mean the little stuff, like shooting a par four on the golf course, making a flaming baked Alaska cake for a birthday party, or choosing the right shirt to match the day's outfit. I mean the really important stuff, like teaching a cherished child right from wrong, finding the right home to buy in a tumultuous market, fulfilling a responsibility that impacts your whole community, or even, perhaps, facing a new aspect of your job that requires new skills.

For those enormously important jobs, I—and probably you, too—often feel inadequate. It's a scary feeling to have something expected of you that you are not sure you can do. Find comfort from the great apostle Paul, who found himself in exactly that situation. He had what he called, "a thorn in [the] flesh" (2 Cor. 12:6-7). It might have been a physical handicap or perhaps a bad relationship. At any rate, he felt like he could not possibly do what God had called him to do as long as that thorn was there. He felt it was a messenger sent from Satan to torment him.

Three times, probably in three extended seasons of prayer, Paul prayed that God would take away his handicap. But God, in His wonderful mercy, said, "No, Paul. 'My grace is all you need. My power works best in weakness'" (2 Cor. 12:9).

No, Jesus said, His infirmity was not from Satan; it was from Him, the One Who loved him so much, He died to rescue him. Paul's weakness was actually a blessing from God because it was better to have God's power in the hardest of circumstances than his own puny resources. How did the apostle Paul respond? He said he'd be glad to be so weak, just so he would have the power of the Lord Jesus in his life!

Here's the story from 2 Corinthians 12:7-10:

> Even though I have received such wonderful revelations from God. So to keep me from becoming proud, I was given a thorn in my flesh, a messenger from Satan to torment me and keep me from becoming proud. Three different times I begged the Lord to take it away. Each time he said, "My grace is all you need. My power works best in weakness." So now I am glad to boast about my weaknesses, so that the power of Christ can work through me. That's why I take pleasure in my weaknesses, and in the insults, hardships, persecutions, and troubles that I suffer for Christ. For when I am weak, then I am strong.

Thank God that when we are weak, we experience the incredible strength and wisdom of Christ in our lives.

12
"If It's Worth Doing, Do It Well?"

D id your mother warn you, "If it's worth doing, do it well?" Then blame the
fourth Earl of Chesterfield. He's the man who said it first, trying to teach
his son "the art of becoming a man of the world and a gentleman."[20]

It's true: God has given us this *now*, this moment of life. It's a limited
commodity. How foolish it would be to fritter it away carelessly. King
Solomon said, "Whatever you do, do well. For when you go to the grave, there
will be no work or planning or knowledge or wisdom" (Eccl. 9:10).

But the things we must do again and again are not the sole reason God put
us here on His earth. They are necessities that enable us to do the important
things God wants us to do. A man must work conscientiously every day to
earn a living; but even at a routine job, he can be a strong encouragement to
his fellow workers. A new mother will have a load of laundry she'll have to
wash again tomorrow. But while she is doing it cheerfully, she can still be
creating a home that will draw her children to Jesus.

But "doing it well" does not mean doing it slowly. Studies have shown, for
example, that people who read fast retain more of what they read than those
who read slowly. In the biography, *Cheaper by the Dozen*, the mother of that
dozen children was Lillian Gilbreth. She earned three Ph.D.'s in engineering
and psychology. She said, "I sought to provide women with shorter, simpler,
and easier ways of doing housework to enable them to seek paid employment
outside the home." She invented the foot pedal trash can and the shelves on

---

20 Philip Dormer Stanhope, *Earl of Chesterfield, Letters to His Son, Complete On the Fine
Art of Becoming a Man of the World and a Gentleman* (Mainz: Gutenberg Press, 2004),
https://www.gutenberg.org/ebooks/3361.

the inside of refrigerator doors. She determined the best height for kitchen counters. She made many other innovations you likely use.21 Looking for the "shorter, simpler, and easier ways of doing housework" can help you do any kind of job well *and* quickly.

But sometimes, when God has burdened me with a serious task, I have felt totally inadequate. I felt I didn't have the skills, the wisdom, or even the time to do it like it ought to be done. But it had to be done, so I did it the best I could. That's when I was comforted by G. K. Chesterton's cheerful statement, "Sometimes anything worth doing is worth doing badly." God can use us despite our weaknesses, or—might it be—because of our weaknesses?

Perhaps the secret is found in Colossians 3:17: "And whatever you do or say, do it as a representative of the Lord Jesus, giving thanks through him to God the Father."

Thank God that He can use us vulnerable, inadequate human beings for His good purposes. No matter what I do each day, routine and boring or challenging and rewarding, I can do it in His name and for His sake. And I won't always know how successful it will turn out to be. I can leave that in God's loving hands.

21   Frank B. Gilbreth and Ernestine Gilbreth Carey, *Cheaper by the Dozen* (New York: Harper Perennial Modern Classics, 2019).

73
Always Trusting, Never Doubting

The refrain of Charles Tindley's sweet gospel song "Take Your Burden to the Lord and Leave It There" has a line in it that troubles me. I couldn't possibly say that I never doubt but rather always trust in the Lord. Why, my heart is often full of misgivings. Sometimes, when I hear bad news, my first thought is not, *I can trust God about this.* My first thought might be, *Oh dear, oh dear, what in the world will happen next?* You can't exactly call that "always trusting," can you?

But when I go to the Scriptures, I learn that God *wants* me to talk to Him about my doubts. He says, "Present your case," like a lawyer argues before a court (Isa. 41:21, 43:26, 45:21). He says, "'Come now, let's settle this,'" (Isa. 1:18). So He certainly isn't angry when I have doubts. He wants me to tell Him all about them.

And in this matter, the Lord Jesus is my best Defense. "For there is one God and one Mediator who can reconcile God and humanity—the man Christ Jesus" (1 Tim. 2:5). When I feel sinful because I am filled with doubt, the Lord Jesus says, "I'm here to make it right with your Heavenly Father. You've got it made!"

The Scriptures record a beautiful incident in Mark 9:15-27 that helps me understand this. A distraught father once brought his little boy to Jesus to be healed of epileptic seizures caused by a demon. He said to Jesus, "'Have mercy on us and help us, if you can'" (v. 22). He hoped Jesus could help him, but he expressed great doubt because of the enormity of the child's affliction.

With deep compassion, Jesus answered his doubts: "'Anything is possible if a person believes'" (v. 23).

Then the Scripture says, "The father instantly cried out, 'I do believe, but help me overcome my unbelief!'" (v. 24).

And of course, we know the outcome: Jesus healed the boy and gave him back to his father.

I take heart from this incident in Christ's life: "Lord, 'help me overcome my unbelief!'" My doubts will not keep me from seeing God's answer to my prayer if I have only enough faith to ask. Doubts become sin only if I make wrong choices because of them.

Yes, take your burden to the Lord and leave it there, even when you doubt. God will deliver you just as He has always promised His beloved children.

74
The "Rice" Way and the Wrong Way

My preacher father invested his life in helping to prepare young men for the ministry by bringing them into our home to live with us for a time. All of us in the Rice family took for granted that there would be guests at the dining table and that we were to make them welcome.

I was probably nine years old when one of the young "preacher boys" offered to help me set the table for supper. The only problem was—and it was a major one, in my young mind—he actually put the knife, fork, and spoon all on the righthand side of the plate when everybody *knows* the fork goes on the left! I told him so in no uncertain terms.

Amusement colored his voice as he said, "Are you sure that's the only way to place the silverware?"

"Yes," I said vehemently. "There are only two ways—the wrong way and the Rice way!"

The "Rice" way may have been the right way for the Rice family to set a table; but I have learned, to my chagrin, that in many families, even in America, it isn't done that way at all! And I would have blanched if I had seen the Queen of England's table set at Windsor Castle, as I recently did. Half-a-dozen forks and spoons were lined up on both sides of the plate, besides the ones positioned at the top of the plate for the desserts and cheese and fruit!

I was wrong at nine years old. And now, in my eighties, I often find, again, that I am wrong about something about which I have a very decided opinion. Do I find it easy to confess this, to say, "I was wrong"? No, hardly ever—especially if it means admitting I'm wrong to my husband or my grown children. I like being right.

Why is it so hard for us to admit that we were wrong about a matter? Shouldn't we be glad to admit that we were wrong and now know the truth about something? I do want to be teachable, and I do want to be wiser tomorrow than I am today. Moses, the prophet, had the humility to pray, "Teach us to realize the brevity of life, so that we may grow in wisdom" (Psalm 90:12). May it be so in my life as well.

75
What Seed Did You Plant Today?

Robert Louis Stevenson said, "Don't judge each day by the harvest you reap, But by the seeds that you plant."[22]

We do reap a harvest, day by day, from seeds planted weeks, even years ago. The results of things we did long ago from decisions we made tend to crop up unexpectedly—some of them good, some of them embarrassing, perhaps even shaming. What shall we do about the harvest of those seeds planted so long ago?

Case in point: a dear woman I've been trying to help has a ten-year-old son who desperately longs to know his father. That's not going to be possible. The man has gotten married, wants no reminders of an illicit relationship, and has no intention of accepting his son into his present life. The heartbroken mother spends her days grieving for the wrong she did to her son, so much so that she is dysfunctional, almost incapacitated. How glad I was to remind her that God says in Romans 5:20, "God's law was given so that all people could see how sinful they were. But as people sinned more and more, God's wonderful grace became more abundant."

No matter how terrible the sin, there is more than enough grace to wipe it out! Christ offers forgiveness and redemption, not just erasing the record but promising a joyful and productive life. That doesn't mean that mother won't have to chop down some of the weeds she planted in years past. She may sometimes have to deal with some of the consequences. But she doesn't

---

22 Robert Louis Stevenson, "Robert Louis Stevenson Quotes," BrainyQuote.com, Accessed June 4, 2024, https://www.brainyquote.com/quotes/robert_louis_stevenson_101230.

have to focus on the sadness of the past. She can build a serene and loving home atmosphere for her son now, teaching him, enjoying him, broadening his relationships, preparing him for the future God wants him to have.

God's Word says, "Consider the farmers who patiently wait for the rains in the fall and in the spring. They eagerly look for the valuable harvest to ripen. You, too, must be patient. Take courage, for the coming of the Lord is near" (James 5:7-8).

So how profitable will today be? Don't judge it by the harvest you reap. Judge it by how well you plant honest and good seed and wait patiently for the wonderful harvest!

76
Why Doesn't God Do Something?

Years ago, my husband and I were walking through the Ford Museum in Dearborn when he stopped me by a huge Farmall F-20 tractor.

"There," Walt said, "that's the tractor I bought last week. They'll deliver it next week."

You understand, Walt was delighted to be serving God in a church. It was what he'd given his life to. But he also had a wide swathe of farmer in his city-bred heart. We owned a half-acre of land next to our home, and he thought he'd raise a big garden on it. The only problem was that this huge tractor he'd bought had such a wide turning radius, he couldn't even circle once in that cramped half-acre.

Undaunted, he rented a field down the road from our home. He plowed it and planted corn on it. The very next morning, he got up early and dug up some of the kernels of corn to see if the corn had sprouted yet! But a farmer has to wait. Walt knew—from the instructions on the package of seed corn—exactly how many days it would take for the corn to ripen at our latitude. There's a time for sowing and a time for reaping, a time of waiting scheduled by God Himself (Eccl. 3).

Mark 4:26-29 talks about the experience of one farmer:

> Jesus also said, "The Kingdom of God is like a farmer who scatters seed on the ground. Night and day, while he's asleep or awake, the seed sprouts and grows, but he does not understand how it happens. The earth produces the crops on its own. First a leaf blade pushes through, then the heads of wheat are formed,

and finally the grain ripens. And as soon as the grain is ready, the farmer comes and harvests it with a sickle, for the harvest time has come."

The farmer didn't know how it all worked, but he knew when the harvest was ready. In the same way, we human beings often expect God to act immediately. If He doesn't, we accuse Him of breaking His promise.

A mother recently told me she was disappointed with God. Her son was not living for God as they had taught him.

"I pray, but nothing happens. Why doesn't God do something?"

But how could she know what God was doing inside that young man's heart? Psalm 119:68 says, "You are good and do only good; teach me your decrees." God cannot, and will not, do anything to hurt His children. If we can't *see* Him acting in our behalf, that's no indication of what He is doing underneath.

A businessman commits himself to a venture that should prosper; but despite his prayers and wise decisions, nothing seems to develop. Perhaps the seed has not had time to germinate.

A woman volunteers to teach a Bible study. She works and prays diligently as she prepares the lessons. But she doesn't see much impact. Might it be God is working in the hearts of the women but not in ways she can see?

A student might spend hours researching for a paper that doesn't impress his professor. But might it be God is teaching him some profound truths that will shape the rest of his life?

Ecclessiates 3:11 says, "Yet God has made everything beautiful for its own time. He has planted eternity in the human heart, but even so, people cannot see the whole scope of God's work from beginning to end."

Our humanity may keep us from understanding all that God is doing for us. We may not be able to see how He is working in the hearts of others. But we can be sure that God will make everything turn out for our good, exactly when we need it. And He will do it in His perfect time.

77
Are You Audit Ready?

Forms 1040 for income taxes were due last week. I dutifully filled out all the information on my software program, and I checked and rechecked my figures. I read the warning that when I clicked on the icon to send, my file would be irretrievable; so did I need to check it again? I resolutely clicked on the icon to send, and my taxes were done for the year.

Or were they?

There's a sign in front of a business on Pelham Road that has asked me for months, "Are you audit ready?" I ignored the sign in July. I smiled at it in September. I frowned at it in March. But this April, it startled me. I asked myself, seriously, "Am I audit ready?"

I filed a 1040 form with my husband every year for sixty-seven years. We were audited twice, two years in a row. It was a scary thing, but it turned out everything was in good order. Since I could be one of the random audits the IRS makes this year, I have kept every receipt, every bank record, every bit of information they might request. IRS audits are plain nerve-wracking.

But that sign on Pelham Road keeps asking me, "Are you audit ready?" It reminds me that there is another audit for which I need to be prepared. I need to be sure that there's no outstanding balance I still owe, no warrant out for my arrest. It's a question that troubles every one of us human beings, no matter how old we are or what accounting system we use. We must answer to God for our moral decisions.

One day, the Bible says, there will be an audit. I'll stand before God, and He'll have His account book open. He'll look to see if I have an unpaid balance, some kind of failure with which I've been charged. What will He find on that judgment day? Nothing! Not a blot, not an accusation, not a charge, thank God!

It's not because I've done everything right. If you knew me, you'd know better than that. And God certainly knows how often I fail. But because the Lord Jesus took my penalty for me and paid the price for my sin by His death on the cross, I don't have to fear God's audit. My account is clear. My penalty has been paid. I am right with God because Jesus took my sin away and gave me His righteousness. I'm audit-ready.

You can be audit ready, too. Here's the Scripture that explains how:

> So now there is no condemnation for those who belong to Christ Jesus. And because you belong to him, the power of the life-giving Spirit has freed you from the power of sin that leads to death. The law of Moses was unable to save us because of the weakness of our sinful nature. So God did what the law could not do. He sent his own Son in a body like the bodies we sinners have. And in that body God declared an end to sin's control over us by giving his Son as a sacrifice for our sins. He did this so that the just requirement of the law would be fully satisfied for us, who no longer follow our sinful nature but instead follow the Spirit (Rom. 8:1-4).

Are you audit-ready—not just this tax season but for eternity? You can be by taking God's gift of forgiveness through Jesus. All we have to do is give Him all our IOUs for our sins and accept the gift of His righteousness. Now that's a wonderful audit guarantee!

78
God Is Still in Control

Sweat trickled down my back as the FAA inspector said to me, "Okay, Mrs. Handford, take us back to Greenville." I turned the little Cessna 150 southwest back toward home. My flight exam for my private pilot's license was over. What would be his verdict? Of course I was tense. This man would determine whether I was good enough a pilot to be trusted with others' lives.

The Greenville Downtown airport is the busiest general aviation airport in South Carolina, so radio communications with the tower that day were very crowded. I had to wait several minutes before I could ask for permission to land. I heard they were using runway three-six.

I keyed the mike. "Greenville tower," I radioed, "Cessna 3601Victor inbound from the east for landing at GMU."

The controller said, "3601Victor, enter a left base for runway one-eight."

Runway one-eight? But one-eight faced south; it was the same as runway three-six but the opposite end. I was confused. If I landed on runway one-eight, I'd run straight into all the other planes he'd cleared to land on three-six.

Trying to control the tremor in my voice, I said, "Greenville tower, Cessna 3601Victor, I didn't hear you well. Please say again."

"Great call," the inspector said to me quietly. "You have a right to question any instruction you don't understand. He's made a mistake."

All the planes on the frequency were in peril, so they crowded on the radio to confirm their own instructions. The radio was silent for a moment. Then a new voice came on. Someone had taken charge up in that tower. He seemed to know where every plane was. He had a clear plan for each of us, what to do and in what order.

His voice was deep and authoritative. "3601Victor, enter a right downwind for runway three-six. All other aircraft stand by." Then he gave instructions to each pilot on the frequency, giving clear and precise instructions.

If you're interested, we all did land safely that day; and the FAA inspector did sign me off for my pilot's license.

Sometimes, in my life, the panic I felt that day rushes over me again. I don't know what to do. What should I do? What can I do? It isn't just the personal problems that threaten my family; it's the frightening chaos of a world in rebellion against God. Our country is so divided, so alienated, there seems no hope for a workable unity. Conflicts threaten to become worldwide wars. An enemy country threatens an armed nuclear weapon orbiting the earth. Forecasts of worldwide famine and disease linger. The radioed commands we hear from world leaders are garbled, conflicting, impossible to fulfill.

But there's Someone in the control tower of the universe Who really is in control. He has a flight plan for everyone in His universe, and He will fulfill it. He's King of all kings, and Lord of all lords. What He determines "will be done on earth, as it is in heaven" (Matt. 6:10). This is the message He gave to His disciples (and to us) the night before He gave His life for us: "I have told you all this so that you may have peace in me. Here on earth you will have many trials and sorrows. But take heart, because I have overcome the world" (John 16:33).

Your great, omnipotent God is in charge of His universe. Be of good cheer. You don't need to be afraid anymore.

79
Thinking Critically or Critical Thinking?

As we've watched the news these past few weeks, our daughter reminded us of something her father had taught her in high school.

"Daddy taught me what a difference there is," she said, "between thinking critically and carefully and just being critical."

Ruth was a junior in the Christian high school our church started and on the debate team. Her father was the debate coach. They went to Charlotte to participate in an area-wide high school debate tournament. Ruth, who incidentally really is a good thinker and a good speaker now, felt like she and her partner had demolished their opponents. She bubbled with enthusiasm waiting for the judges' decision, expecting her father to congratulate her for her beautiful job of annihilation. The decision was handed down. They had lost!

Ruth realized her mistake in hindsight. "See, I had picked up on the little things, the non-essentials, their way of saying things. I didn't try to hear what they actually said and speak to that. It sure is easy to believe you are thinking right when you're really just being critical."

Proverbs 18:13 has an interesting observation about this: "Spouting off before listening to the facts is both shameful and foolish." Have I sometimes assumed I knew what a colleague was going to say and expressed my opinion about it before she even said it? Have I concentrated on a person's odd pronunciation of a word or a lisp and so discounted what he was actually saying? Do I have certain "code red" words that if a speaker uses them, I automatically categorize the speaker?

It's a bad habit, as the Scripture says. It is foolish and dangerous. We need clear thinking and clear responses in every part of our lives: in business, in friendships, in our homes, in church, and yes, in politics. Proverbs 9:9 says, "Instruct the wise, and they will be even wiser. Teach the righteous, and they will learn even more."

80
Finishing Is Better Than Starting

The day I received a signed book contract from Zondervan Publishers for my first novel, I was delirious with excitement. I was an author—a paid author! That very day I sat down and outlined another fiction story. It would be so good. It would probably be a best-seller. I could hardly wait to get it written and sent to Zondervan. They'd be impressed that they had a full-fledged, serious author on their hands. (Yes, I know, I was naïve!)

I'm embarrassed to confess that that second marvelous book (which you never heard of) didn't make its appearance until forty-five years later. Oh, I dabbled with it, and I wrote some other things. But the story I conceived with such enthusiasm moldered in my head, and I did not complete it until recently. (If you should happen to be interested after this tedious introduction, it's called *I Am Dying of Thirst by the Fountain*, a love story of loss and redemption, available in Kindle format and print on Amazon.)

Joan Miró was a Spanish painter and sculptor who died in 1983. He was a surrealist. That's not my most favorite art style; and I confess that I don't understand his paintings, even when he gives them a title! But he was a successful and tremendously careful craftsman. He said, "The works must be conceived with fire in the soul, but executed with clinical coolness."[23]

I had a dream of a novel I would write. It was a "fire in my soul." But I did not execute it with "clinical coolness." I didn't "execute" it at all. My dream

---

23 "Summary of Joan Miró," The Art Story, Accessed July 25, 2024, https://www.theartstory.org/artist/miro-joan.

could not turn into reality until I carefully and methodically set about getting it down on paper.

A brilliant idea is only the first step in accomplishing something valuable and important. Many a wonderful business concept has failed—not because it was flawed but because its owner failed to follow through with the hard work of putting it into shape.

King Solomon said in Ecclesiastes 7:8, "Finishing is better than starting. Patience is better than pride." Could it be that the dream you have of doing something wonderful for God with your life needs to be looked at, pondered over, and faithfully, day after day, put into shape? That vision you had about your job, that truly important and needed vision, does it languish because your enthusiasm cooled at the hard work ahead? That sweet home you envisioned for your children, that enduring relationship you intended to give them, has it become a burden because, as Miró said, it required more "clinical coolness" than you had expected?

God's answer to all this is found in 1 Corinthians 15:58: "So, my dear brothers and sisters, be strong and immovable. Always work enthusiastically for the Lord, for you know that nothing you do for the Lord is ever useless."

81
God Says, "Let's Have a Conversation"

Our daughter Ruth came to live with us when she was three months old. My mother drove us home from the adoption agency that day, since Walt was away on a preaching mission. That dear child lay in my arms and talked to me and her new big brother John the whole way home. Sometimes, she explained something very earnestly; sometimes, she chuckled with glee or jabbered. But on that hour-long drive home, without knowing a single word, she communicated eloquently with me every mile of the way.

When she was about four years old, she came in from playing outside and said, "Mother, let's have a 'commeration.'"

"All right, dear. What shall we 'commerate' about?"

She began the conversation by telling me what was on her heart. And my mother-heart was so tender toward her as we "commerated" together. That was what I had longed for—that sweet and intimate relationship—during all those long years that Walt and I had prayed so earnestly for a child.

Her conversations with me even now are just as precious. In fact, I love my "commerations" with all of my adult children today.

Psalm 27:8 says, "My heart has heard you say, 'Come and talk with me.' And my heart responds, 'Lord, I am coming.'" In this Psalm, the eternal, holy, omnipotent God asks you to please come and talk with Him! Why do you suppose He would want to spend His precious time with us when He has all the universes to keep track of? You might think He wouldn't want to "hang out" with somebody as unimportant as you and I. But King David says plainly that he heard God say to him, "Please come and talk with me. There are so many things I want to share with you." It is an invitation to you from your Creator, Who created you so He could give you all the treasures of Heaven. He fashioned you on purpose to be His friend, His intimate companion.

What would He say to you in that kind of an intimate conversation? He would tell you how much He loves you, how He longs to meet your needs and comfort you in the hard things of life. He would tell you that He knows all about your sins and that His Son Jesus died so your debt could be erased, if only you'll take His gift. He'd tell you that you could actually hear His voice speaking to you as you read His book, the Bible.

And what would you talk to Him about in that intimate conversation? You could tell Him how grateful you are for His love and forgiveness. You could ask Him for wisdom in the difficult decisions you have to make day by day. You could tell Him all about your fears and heartaches. You could talk together about the hundred things real friends talk about.

That's why God says, "Come and talk with Me."

How I hope your heart answer will be, "Lord, I am coming."

82
Our Above-Average Children and Report Card Woes

Garrison Keillor used to say, "Welcome to Lake Wobegon, where all the women are strong, all the men are goodlooking, and all the children are above average."[24] Maybe not all the women in our town are strong, nor all the men good-looking, but everybody knows our children really are above average!

Time magazine recently reported that 90 percent of all American parents believe their children are intellectually above average.[25] Since that is obviously impossible, it predicts that many parents are doomed to disappointment on report cards days; and just as surely, their children will be frustrated and embarrassed.

I remember when one of our children came home with a really poor report card. I tried to comfort her by saying, "Honey, when you get out of school, there won't be any more report cards. People will judge you on what you can do, not what you made on a test."

But that's only partly true. Most of us undergo evaluation of some kind from time to time at our jobs. And all of us have relationships with people whose expectations of us are high.

What brings this to mind is that last week a young friend of mine got the results of a test she took to confirm college credit for an AP high school course. She's a wonderful athlete, a sweet Christian with heaps of friends,

---

24 Garrison Keillor, "Inside Garrison Keillor's fabled world of 'A Prairie Home Companion,'" July 26, 2014, in *PBS News Hour*, Radio, 10:37, https://www.pbs.org/newshour/show/40-years-counting-inside-garrison-keillors-fabled-world-prairie-home-companion#transcript.
25 Jenny Anderson, "Many American Parents Have No Idea How Their Kids Are Doing in School," *Time*, August 28, 2023, https://time.com/6308834/american-parents-how-their-kids-doing-in-school/.

and has a great grade-point average. She's not accustomed to failure. But she didn't make the grade, and she was devastated.

I've told you before how wonderful my parents were. But I have to say in this regard, my father was so smart, he was able to master information easily. Because learning was so easy for him, he really did think that if you were a good Christian, if you really worked at it, you could make straight A's! As loving and kind a father as he was, he wasn't very patient when a C plus showed up on a report card. He just knew you could do better if you tried harder!

Perhaps you remember some failure of yours like that. It may be that the memory still rankles. Perhaps you still chafe because you couldn't meet your parents' expectations. It may be you sometimes face challenges at work that seem beyond your ability to master, and old feelings of inadequacy come back to haunt you.

It's time to remind ourselves how God feels about all this. Jeremiah 9:23-24 says, "'Let not the wise boast of their wisdom or the strong boast of their strength or the rich boast of their riches, but let the one who boasts boast about this: that they have the understanding to know me, that I am the Lord, who exercises kindness, justice and righteousness on earth, for in these I delight,' declares the Lord."

We did not choose our abilities and talents, though, of course, we should work at developing them. But we can choose to "boast in this alone" that we understand and know Him. When we do, we delight our God. And we can accomplish more for God's kingdom than someone far more intellectually gifted but less committed.

Where should we find our self-worth? What should we brag about? The answer is not our accomplishments, not our talents, nor our wealth. Instead, let's thank God that we can know Him as our dearest Friend, that He reveals His heart to us so we can understand what He is doing. Compared to that, it really doesn't seem too important whether we graduated with average grades or were a valedictorian. Oh, yes! We know Jesus, and that's enough!

83
What's My Most Important Task Today?

In the 1930s, my father moved to an impoverished section of Dallas to take the gospel to people no one else seemed to care about. Many came to Christ; and with their volunteer labor and unselfish giving, they built a modest building. Soon after they moved into it, someone noticed smoke curling from the back wall during a morning service. Firemen fought the blaze while church members worked frantically to save the furniture and office equipment. Daddy, distraught at seeing his dream going up in flames, grabbed some boxes of cheap greeting cards to save from the fire. In his haste, he spilled them. As he scrambled to pick them up, someone yelled, "Pastor, leave that stuff! Save the expensive Bibles!"

An economist named Pareto discovered that in the inventory of a business, about 80 percent of the value lies in 20 percent of the items. He called that 20 percent "the vital few." An illustration of this idea is the little bits of merchandise at Walmart like pencils and string and buttons make up about 80 percent of their inventory, but they're worth only 20 percent of the inventory value. Big ticket items like TVs and computers comprise about 20 percent of their stock, but they are worth about 80 perecent of the total investment.[26] If we applied this principle at work, could it be that if we took care of the most important things, "the vital few," we might accomplish 80 percent of the job?

26   John Black, Niger Hashimzade, and Gareth Myles, *A Dictionary of Economics*, (Oxford: Oxford University Press, 2009), https://www.oxfordreference.com/display/10.1093/acref/9780199237043.001.0001/acref-9780199237043-e-3816.

Microsoft did this. They analyzed the reports of malfunctions in their computer software. When they fixed the first 20 perecent of all complaints about system bugs, they found they had solved 80 percent of them.[27]

You say, "Good idea, Libby. But it sounds complicated."

Maybe not. Often, when I'm dealing with an important assignment, I try to clear the deck. I try to dispose of all those little, niggling undone tasks so I can focus on the important job at hand. What happens too often is that at the end of the day, I still have a handful of less important tasks generated by my "clearing the deck"; and I have not touched the truly important thing I was hired to do.

What is your truly important "vital few"? It's probably fairly easy to determine at work. If you are not sure, check your job description. Your supervisor can certainly clarify it for you.

It may be harder to determine the vital 20 percent in your personal life. That takes clear-headed thinking and wisdom from God. Some things really can wait until tomorrow. Some really must be done today; and sometimes, trivial things are still essential. Whatever you do, don't leave undone the thing that matters most!

Jesus tackled this problem when He said in Matthew 6:31-32, "So don't worry about these things, saying, *What will we eat? What will we drink? What will we wear?* These things dominate the thoughts of unbelievers, but your heavenly Father already knows all your needs."

Jesus is promising that He knows all about the nitty-gritty stuff of life, and He'll see about them while you work on the vital 20 percent. What are the vital few? "'Seek the Kingdom of God above all else, and live righteously, and he will give you everything you need'" (Matt. 6:33). That means honoring Him in every decision and every action. When I do that, God promises He'll take care of everything else!

---

27 Nagabhushanam Peddi, "Unleashing the Power of the Pareto Principle in Entrepreneurship," Startup Savant, July 2, 2024, https://startupsavant.com/startup-basics/pareto-principle-in-entrepreneurship#:~:text=Software%20 giant%20Microsoft%20once%20discovered%20through%20its%20research,top%20 issues%2C%20maximizing%20user%20satisfaction%20with%20fewer%20fixes.

84
Idiopathic

Long ago, I sat in my dentist's chair as he probed my mouth. We'd always had interesting conversations. But he had one very bad habit. If I disagreed with him and started burbling my opinion, he would fill my mouth with cotton or blobs of something so that I couldn't maintain my side of the argument. This happened the morning I asked him if he would trust Jesus as his Savior.

A month later, after Walt had led him to the Lord, I asked him if he'd stuffed my mouth on purpose to stop my asking, and he said, "Yes."

Once he commented on the odd-shaped Mandibular Tori in my jaw. "It's a good thing you haven't needed a partial plate," he said. "Those would sure complicate fitting it."

"What causes them?"

"They're idiopathic."

"What does that mean?"

"I don't know."

When I could talk past his instruments, I protested, "Why in the world would you use a word when you don't even know what it means?"

"I do know what it means," he said reasonably. "It means 'I don't know.'"

There's a word in the English language that I could use to confess I'm not the dispenser of all wisdom? Well, yes, there is: *idiopathic*. Though it's actually a medical term, I need to learn to use it more often in my relationships with others.

We mothers are very accustomed to being right about everything when we talk with our children. No, I didn't say that right. I should say that mothers *think* they are always right when they're talking to their children. Actually, I've discovered, not only do my children know about things I know nothing about, like navigating the internet; but also, they are often right about human relationships and matters of right and wrong. I should listen to them.

As a pastor's wife, I discovered that the people God sent to my husband and me to nurture spiritually often had a clearer insight into a certain passage of Scripture than I did. If I were really wise, I would say, "I don't know."

When I was the young office manager of my father's Christian book publishing company, I was managing many older, accomplished, smart employees, people who did their jobs well. I quickly learned that I needed to be teachable about many procedures. I didn't need to be the "know-it-all" solver of all the problems that crop up in a business. I wouldn't lose their respect when I said, "I don't know; and if you don't know, we'll find out together."

In Psalm 90:12, the prophet Moses prayed, "Teach us to realize the brevity of life, so that we may grow in wisdom." King Solomon said in Proverbs 23:23, "Get the truth and never sell it; also get wisdom, discipline, and good judgment."

I have learned what I especially need to say to my Father God when I'm trying to figure out why I've missed the mark in my relationship with Him. "I don't know why that happened, dear Lord. I'm listening to what You want me to hear, and then I'll obey You as fast as I can."

85
God's Sweet Surprise

Have you ever suddenly awakened in the night and remembered with shame something you'd done years before, something you'd forgotten all about? That happened to me the other night.

I am a child of the Depression era of the 1930s, when one-fourth of all Americans were out of a job and many more were earning barely enough to keep food on the table. I remember men selling pencils on the streets for a nickel, people knocking on our door begging for something to eat, Christians at church tearfully asking for prayer to find a job.

The church Daddy pastored was in the poorest section of Dallas. Our only income came from the "love offerings" of our impoverished church members. My dear mother coped valiantly to feed our family and whoever else unexpectedly showed up at our table. She would fry salmon patties, mixing a can of inexpensive salmon with an egg and an onion and enough breadcrumbs to make servings for ten. Or she would take a link of bologna or a can of SPAM, chop it into small pieces, and serve it in white sauce on toast for a meal for our big family.

At one of those lovingly planned meager meals, I—maybe eight years old at the time—had the gall to say something like, "Well, Mother, this sure isn't very much of a meal."

Mother should have sent me to my room with a promise of no supper. Instead, with tears in her eyes, she simply said, "But I have a very special surprise for you—I have vanilla ice cream for dessert!"

And it *was* a special, wonderful surprise. We had only an ice box, not a refrigerator with a freezer; so ice cream was a rare treat.

I share this humiliating memory because you may need the reminder, as I do, that some of God's sweetest surprises are still ahead. I know why God brought to my mind this embarrassing childhood incident. I have been feeling a little disappointed with God. Oh, don't misunderstand, I am the grateful recipient of His constant care, His unfailing supply, day after day, year after year. My God has been supremely generous with me all my life. But there is one important thing God has not given me, something I feel I desperately need. When He is so generous with me in so many, many ways, why doesn't He, in His power and authority, give me this?

That's when I remembered my mother's response to my arrogant complaint: "I have a very special surprise for you—I have ice cream for dessert!"

Is that God's answer to my selfish complaint? "I have a very, very special surprise for you; and you'll love it, but you'll have to wait for it."

In fact, God has clear instructions for me in Psalm 27:14: "Wait patiently for the LORD. Be brave and courageous. Yes, wait patiently for the LORD."

So I must wait for God to do, in His good time, exactly what He knows will satisfy the longings of my heart. It may not necessarily be what I've been asking for because He knows my heart better than I do. Someday, I will thank Him because He gave me what I really needed, not what I asked for. His plan for me really will meet every desire of my heart.

When I have the courage to say, "God, I want your will, not mine," my heart will be strengthened. Then I can wait patiently. And whatever His will is in this specific matter, it will be more wonderful even than home-churned vanilla ice cream!

86
Compromise Isn't Always Bad

As a child in Texas, I remember being taught to never, ever compromise. ("Remember the Alamo!") Texans always stand for what's right. And soberly, as an adult, I really do want to stand for what's right. But the truth I've learned is that good people can have valid arguments for opposing views. That's happening in America today, and it is tearing our dear country apart. The quarrels are brutal and rude. Our politicians seem unable to listen to each other and find a way to resolve conflicts. There was a time in the history of our country when we nearly lost every precious freedom we'd won in the Revolution. Our founding fathers were standing on principle. They could not see a way to reconcile truly valid, differing concerns.

The year was 1787. We'd fought the war with England to stop King George III from imposing unfair taxes. The peace treaty with England had been signed. Now American patriots gathered in Philadelphia to write a constitution for this new nation. Every citizen would have a voice in government. But how were they to accomplish that? The large, populous colonies didn't want the small ones to have too much power; the small ones feared being controlled by the large, populous colonies. Debates, day after day, did not resolve the problem. Fear and anger threatened to end the congress, and that would end all hope for a *United* States.

Then Benjamin Franklin stood up. "Friends," he said quietly, "too much is at stake here to continue this quarrel. I ask you, each one, to go home and pray. Pray earnestly that God will give us the wisdom to solve this problem. Gentlemen, go home and pray!" And they did.[28]

Ecclesiastes 8:5-6 says, "Those who obey him will not be punished. Those who are wise will find a time and a way to do what is right, for there is a time and a way for everything, even when a person is in trouble."

After humbling themselves and praying, the delegates returned to Philadelphia. Roger Sherman and Oliver Ellsworth offered the Connecticut Compromise. It proposed a bicameral house of two chambers. The House of Representatives would have members in proportion to their state's population. The Senate would have two senators from each state, regardless of size or population. Checks and balances between the Congress, the president, and the Supreme Court would help to prevent any of the three from gaining too much power. It was an elegant solution, a miracle of fair government, unlike anything the world had ever seen. It was accomplished with humility and prayer.

As God has helped us in the past, may He help our leaders again to humbly find ways to solve the conflicts shredding our dear country. It can be done but only if we humble ourselves and pray. Yes, it can be done. Come to think of it, couldn't many of the conflicts in homes, businesses, churches, and governments be settled with fair and ethical compromise?

---

28   Bowen, ibid.

87
Like What You Have To Do

I was caring for a child whose mother had suddenly abandoned her family. The father was desperately looking for ways to make sure the children were cared for, so that day I watched the five-year-old while the two older children were in school.

At the lunch table, the little boy said, "My tummy hurts," and he ran for the bathroom. I wasn't surprised that the child was upset. His mother had disappeared without telling him goodbye, and his whole world had turned upside down.

I heard him vomiting, so I ran toward the bathroom to help him. In my haste, I didn't see the mess he'd made on the bathroom floor. I skidded across the room, skinned my knees, and found myself covered with yucky slime. The child stood with absolute terror on his face. I realized he was afraid of how I would react.

I picked myself up and grinned at him. "I was showing off. Pretty good, huh? Here, honey, let me get you cleaned up. I'll give you something to settle your tummy, and you can take a nap."

I put him in clean clothes and tucked the covers around him. He sighed a tentative smile and went to sleep. Then I tackled the mess in the bathroom and cleaned myself up. And somehow, I didn't feel the disgust I'd expected. It almost seemed like holy ground because I was helping a frightened little boy for Jesus' sake.

The truth is, every task of life has some part of drudgery and boredom, no matter the glamour of the paycheck or the fulfillment of a job well done.

For years, I sobbed out my heart to God, asking Him to give me a baby. When at long last, I held that sweet child in my arms, how was I to know that motherhood came with a package of things I'd have to do that I wouldn't enjoy? How many things did you do today, not because you wanted to do them, certainly not because they were important or enjoyable, but simply because they had to be done?

The Word of God tells us the Lord Jesus stripped Himself of His garments in order to perform that lowliest of a slave's tasks, washing the dirty, smelly, sweaty feet of twelve men too proud to do the task for each other.

When Jesus was done, He said, "'You call me *Teacher* and *Lord*, and you are right, because that's what I am. And since I, your Lord and Teacher, have washed your feet, you ought to wash each other's feet. I have given you an example to follow. Do as I have done to you" (John 13:13-15). Then He added the words that can forever make lowly tasks endurable: "'Now that you know these things, God will bless you for doing them'" (John 13:17).

That makes it so I can't use the word "important" or "unimportant" to describe each task God has given me to do each day. If I am doing exactly what God told me to do, I will find joy and fulfillment even in the most unsavory, dreariest job. Jesus promises such a sweet reward to those who complete lowly tasks simply because they are following Him. Matthew 10:42 42 says, "And if you give even a cup of cold water to one of the least of my followers, you will surely be rewarded."

If you love the Lord Jesus and tackle even the most distasteful task because you love Him, God notes it well and reserves a special reward for you. And that makes the lowliest, most difficult task a holy task. And that, dear friend, is why you can learn to like doing whatever God has given you to do today.

88
When Somebody Hurts, We Say, "I Care"

When I had a speaking engagement in Guam, I fell at the church and broke my hand. The doctor put a psychedelic neon-pink cast on my arm and hand and said I'd be fine. But the long flight across the Pacific alone was irritating and tedious because I couldn't even open my bag of peanuts or tie my shoes by myself! The flight attendant put my carry-on in the bin for me, and I settled down to cope as best I could.

But as the plane landed at Atlanta, a man several rows behind me opened the overhead bin, pulled down my carry-on, and said, "I'll carry it into the terminal for you."

"Thanks," I said gratefully, "but how did you know I was going to need help?"

He smiled. "I saw where the flight attendant put your bag. It's very hard to miss a bright pink cast like that!"

I got to wondering how many other people on that jumbo jet were wounded—maybe not physically but spiritually and emotionally—and I didn't know it because they weren't wearing a neon-pink cast. Yet those wounded people needed tenderness and understanding even more than I did. It may be that those who most needed it had hardened their faces to keep from being hurt more by the carelessness of others.

Once when our son John was about eight years old, he came into the kitchen where I was standing at the stove cooking supper. He tugged at my skirt. "Mother, I hurt my finger."

Preoccupied with getting supper on the table for those seven kids, I glanced at his finger. "It's not so bad," I said distractedly. "You'll be fine."

"Mother," he said, aggrieved, "when I tell you I hurt myself, you are supposed to say, 'Oh, John, I'm so sorry. Let's put a Band-Aid on it.'"

He was right, you know. When somebody is hurt, we're supposed to care! Today, with God's help, I am going to try to see people as He looks at them—with compassion and an eagerness to help, whatever their need. As 1 Thessalonians 5:14 reminds us, "Encourage those who are timid. Take tender care of those who are weak."

89
Focusing on the Incidentals Instead of the Essentials

The time was 1931, at the height of the Depression. The place was Fort Worth, Texas, the center of the "Dust Bowl," a time of terrible drought. The Rice family, including five little girls, was moving from Fort Worth to Dallas; and I'm afraid we looked something like the "Okies" in Steinbeck's *The Grapes of Wrath*.

The moving van had left with the furniture. We climbed into the Ford, loaded with all the peripherals a family of seven needed. Then Daddy tied Olga, our nanny goat for milk for baby Joanna, onto the running board. We made a stop by the real estate office to leave the key for the old house, and we were ready for adventure on the marvelous, two-lane turnpike from Fort Worth to Dallas.

When things had settled down, Mother called back to Grace, "How's the baby?"

Startled, Grace said, "Mother, I don't have the baby."

We had loaded the goat for Joanna's milk allergies but forgotten to bring Joanna!

You can imagine our consternation as Daddy drove back to Fort Worth. The house was all locked up except for a window over the kitchen sink. I was the only child old enough to climb through it and able to unlock the front door and still small enough to get through the tiny window. The sight I saw from that little window is etched on my heart forever. Baby Joanna was sitting on the floor, her little fists pumping, crying her heart out.

The apostle Paul well knew the dangers of focusing on the incidentals instead of the essential. He said in Philippians 3:13 that he knew he hadn't already accomplished his goal, and then he said in verse fourteen, "I press on to reach the end of the race and receive the heavenly prize for which God, through Christ Jesus, is calling us."

How often do I focus, not on the essential purpose of my work but on some peripheral object? How often do I worry about the appearance of my child instead of his heart needs? How concerned am I about my "image" in the eyes of other people, rather than enjoying them for themselves?

Oh, yes, dear friends, while we're loading Olga the goat onto the running board of the Ford, let's be sure to tuck sweet little Joanna inside!

90
Our Very Own Thirsty River Birch Tree

I'd never even seen a river birch until Walt and I moved to South Carolina. When I saw my first one, my heart was completely smitten! The patches of dusky pink bark that peeled off were big enough to write a love letter on. Its graceful limbs dripped with green leaves that changed to bright yellow in the fall. Twenty years later, Walt and I bought a home with a river birch tree, and we never tired of that lovely tree that graced our front yard.

But three years of extreme drought came to South Carolina. I noticed no difference in the tree in those three years. It didn't occur to me that the underground water table that had kept the tree green all those years was so diminished that our river birch was getting no water. Of course, it died.

We made a hasty trip to a tree nursery and brought home another river birch. It flourishes regally and greenly in our front yard. And if drought comes again, I will personally and methodically water that tree. Its very name tells me it has to have water to survive. Why didn't I realize that?

It's the same reason my doctor tells me I am dehydrated and need to drink more water. Water is essential for the human body. So why don't I notice when I'm thirsty?

That's even truer in my spiritual life in my relationship with the Lord Jesus. Some days, I am so intent on pushing my way through the day, checking things off my "to do" list, I don't even realize my heart is starving for the presence of God. How can I do anything of value for those I love if I don't have His wisdom, help, and protection? He is there for me, waiting for me to come to Him. Yes, spiritual drought comes into every human heart. When it does, the only answer is to come to Him.

God promises in Isaiah 58:11, "The Lord will guide you continually, giving you water when you are dry and restoring your strength. You will be like a well-watered garden, like an ever-flowing spring." My life as a Christian can flourish, even in times of spiritual drought, if I seek His guidance and meditate on His Word. I can claim this promise of blessing not just for myself but also for my children, their children, and my great-grandchildren. I have a right to ask that of God because that's what He promised in Isaiah 44:3: "For I will pour out water to quench your thirst and to irrigate your parched fields. And I will pour out my Spirit on your descendants, and my blessing on your children."

So when those times of dryness of soul come, thank God He promises "to irrigate your parched fields." We need never to thirst spiritually when we've come to Jesus for eternal life.

91
When the Job Gets Tedious

The job you eagerly trained for, the job you asked God to give you, the job you thought you'd be happy doing for the rest of your life—suddenly, it isn't much fun anymore. We're talking about the job by which you earn your living. But we're also talking about all the important parts of your lifework, the thing you do you feel God created you to do: taking care of people, raising a family, being a friend, ministering to the spiritual needs of others, leaving a legacy in this needy world.

And now that task, whatever it was, has lost its spice and its appeal. You find yourself coping with difficult people. The challenges you met with such hope now seem unattainable. The needed funding isn't there. The emotional cost makes your blood pressure skyrocket. So what should you do when the job gets tedious?

My husband had an interesting way of handling those times in the doldrums. He would go someplace where he could be alone for a while, away from interruptions. Then he'd take out a yellow legal pad, draw a line straight down the middle, head one column "negatives" and the other "positives." In the quietness, Walt would think about his job, analyze it, and identify the frustrating problems. As things came to mind, he'd write it down in the proper column. Sometimes, he would realize that even something truly negative had a positive side, something to be valued. He would evaluate his own performance, consider what impact his handling of things affected how they turned out. He'd write down what had drawn him to the job in the first place and review the reasons he'd decided it was the right fit.

Then, after he'd considered all the pros and cons, he'd meditate on how it seemed God had led him to this specific job and how He had continued to lead him in it. Then he could see that the positives were so positive, the negatives seemed to be less important. Walt would put the pad away to be saved for another attack of tedium. He would take up the task again, assured that this was the place where God had put him, even with its frustrations and disadvantages.

Recently, I asked a man who, I knew, was often frustrated at work by the carelessness of fellow employees, "How do you manage to stay so content at work?"

"The will of God," he said soberly, without further comment.

Boring times, tedious times, difficult times—they come with every job. I suspect even the King of England gets tired of "kinging" sometimes. King Solomon, the wisest of men, observed, "So I saw that there is nothing better for people than to be happy in their work. That is our lot in life. And no one can bring us back to see what happens after we die" (Eccl. 3:22). Ecclesiastes 5:18 expands on that thought: "Even so, I have noticed one thing, at least, that is good. It is good for people to eat, drink, and enjoy their work under the sun during the short life God has given them, and to accept their lot in life."

King Solomon recognized that life is full of hard labor, but he also acknowledges that God is the One Who gave us this labor; and He wants us to enjoy it even in the hard times.

What should I do when my job gets tedious, as it certainly will? I will remember that I am in this place because God has willed it so. And since it is His will, He will give me the wisdom and the patience to do it well for His glory.

92

A Life of Quiet Desperation

Henry David Thoreau said, "The mass of men lead lives of quiet desperation." I know it's true for so many all over the world, struggling just to find food and water and shelter. How often I've tried to help someone with the burdens of just surviving! But I wondered if Thoreau's statement holds true for Christians who love God. Are their lives as quietly desperate as the people who know nothing of God's love and compassion?

I thought of one of my Christian friends who seems to cope with a difficult life with dogged determination, if not exuberance. He works at a very demanding, high-tech job, analyzing and servicing machines critical to manufacturing. His two grown children live far across the country. He has to be away from home much of the time, traveling all over the continent to do his work. He and his wife both have severe health issues, so they have constant financial pressure. Does he live a life of quiet desperation?

I asked him, "What is the hardest thing you face when you go to work each day?"

He answered thoughtfully, "Making sure I do exactly what God wants me to do. So I ask, 'Lord, please show me Your will for today.' And then, all day long, I hear His voice guiding me. Sometimes, it's a hard-to-please customer. Sometimes, it's a malfunctioning machine I need to get back online. Sometimes, it's a problem management needs me to solve. At the end of the day, I feel like I have done what God wanted me to do."

Isaiah was an Old Testament prophet God sent to confront the nation of Israel with their sin. He went through such a time of "quiet desperation."

God had told him, "He said to me, 'You are my servant, Israel, and you will bring me glory'" (Isa. 49:3). But nobody was listening to Isaiah's warnings. Nobody wanted to give up their greed, lust, and selfishness. So Isaiah said to God, "'But my work seems so useless! I have spent my strength for nothing and to no purpose. Yet I leave it all in the Lord's hand; I will trust God for my reward'" (Isa. 49:4).

Quiet desperation, futility—he was a failure, Isaiah thought, trying to use well the one life God had given him to serve Him. But then Isaiah came to the right conclusion: "'Yet I leave it all in the LORD's hand; I will trust God for my reward.'"

But like Isaiah and like my friend expressed so poignantly, I want to know I'm doing what God wants me to do. So God answered Isaiah with comforting authority. "And now the Lord speaks—the one who formed me in my mother's womb to be his servant, who commissioned me to bring Israel back to him. The Lord has honored me, and my God has given me strength" (Isa. 49:5).

So, dear friend, if you struggle with quiet desperation, listen to God's authoritative answer. He made you to serve Him; and you do it all day long by doing the tasks He's given you to do, however mundane and physical they may seem to you. The Lord will honor you, and He will give you the strength you need for today's extraordinary tasks. He promised He would!

93
Close The Gate!

The other day, a service man left my backyard gate open. My little dachshund Schatzi could have easily escaped to the vast, threatening world outside if I had not seen it and closed it.

It reminded me of a day long ago when my father and I were horseback in one of the back pastures on his small farm. His horse, MacArthur, knew exactly what to do when we came to a gate. He stood quietly while Daddy unlatched the gate. We rode through it; and again, MacArthur stood quietly while he latched the gate again.

"Libby," Daddy said earnestly, "always close the gate. If the gate is left open, every cow in the pasture will get out."

A single gate open? And every cow get out? Yes!

There's a parable there.

A woman came to me one day for counsel. Her eyes were red and swollen with tears. "I don't break my marriage vows," she sobbed. "I don't lie. I don't steal. I'm not that kind of woman."

"But—" I asked apprehensively.

"I *am* that kind of woman," she whispered. "It was innocent enough in the beginning. I just flirted with a man at work. And then we started sneaking around, and I lied to my husband. I took money from the petty cash fund at work to cover up what I was spending. Oh, Libby! I'm not that kind of a woman!"

But she was. She left the gate of her heart open, and through that open gate her integrity slipped out and every temptation swarmed into her vulnerable, divided heart. That's why we read in 2 Corinthians 10:3-5, "We are human, but we don't wage war as humans do. We use God's mighty weapons, not worldly weapons, to knock down the strongholds of human reasoning and to destroy false arguments. We destroy every proud obstacle that keeps people from knowing God. We capture their rebellious thoughts and teach them to obey Christ."

Job, the man Satan tried so hard to lead into sin, said, at the height of his temptation, "'I made a covenant with my eye not to look with lust at a young woman'" (Job 31:1). Job said he'd promised himself and God that he would not leave the gate of his heart open to temptation. The gate, left even half-open, makes you vulnerable to every kind of temptation.

But that's not the end of the story, thank God! For He so graciously said, "God's law was given so that all people could see how sinful they were. But as people sinned more and more, God's wonderful grace became more abundant" (Rom. 5:20). God's grace and forgiveness are available to every repentant sinner. So this dear woman came back to Jesus, confessing she was "that kind of woman." She asked His forgiveness and cleansing and set out to live for Him and be the kind of woman she yearned to be.

The moral of this "parable" is if you come to my house, for Schatzi's sake, please keep the gate to the backyard closed. And if, after thinking about it, you should discover the gate of your conscience has been left ajar, talk to the Lord Jesus about it. Fasten it tight, and make a covenant with God to guard it well.

94
The Bitter and Sweet Taste of Vanilla

Polly came to live with us when she was fourteen. Her parents were missionaries in Bolivia, and they felt she needed a better education than they could find for her in the high Andes Mountains. She gave us so much joy the three years she was with us. Every modern convenience we took for granted was a surprise and delight to her. Simple things like the sewing machine, the automatic dishwasher, and the vacuum cleaner all amazed her.

But she especially enjoyed American cooking. One day, we were making a cake from scratch. She'd measured the flour, the shortening, the baking powder, the sugar, and milk. Now it was time to add a tablespoon of vanilla. She measured it out carefully, then put it into the mixture.

"Mmm! That vanilla smells *soooo* good," she said. "Can I taste it?"

"Sure. But you won't like it."

"How could anything that smelled that good not taste delicious?" She poured a spoonful, swallowed it, and shivered involuntarily. "Ugh!"

How many times in my life have I experienced something truly bitter, something I could not understand how a loving God could let happen to me? You've been there. Dreams you've had, promises you've made, people you've loved—sometimes, they seem impossible to realize in the difficulties that surround you. Why does God let it happen when He says He loves us? Could it be that bitter ingredient will someday be part of a wonderful and precious package of love God is preparing for you?

Vanilla alone is bitter. Flour is dry and inedible. Shortening is disgusting. Baking powder is not delicious.! But all of them, in a recipe created by a master chef, mixed together by a baker, can become a delightful birthday party-kind of dessert.

Someone may have glibly quoted Romans 8:28 to you at a time of terrible loss in your life so that its message seems unfeeling. But listen to it in the context of the taste of vanilla:

- "And we know": We know? Yes, we know when things are running smoothly, and we sense God's presence. We're not so sure when things are going badly.
- "God causes everything to work together": Does that include the surprises, failures, betrayals? Do all things work together?
- "For the good": Bad things turn into good in the end when properly mixed? That's what the God Who loves you seems to say. But there is one qualification:
- "Of those who love God": If you love God, if you are His child, then yes, it's true. Nothing, absolutely nothing, can come into your life and hurt you since you have taken Him as your Savior. All the bad stuff—the disappointments, the failures, and the betrayals— God says, "I will take each one of those difficult experiences, and I will shape them into something wonderful in your life."

And at the end, when you see how He has transformed those terrible events in your life into blessings, you will say with joy and confidence, "And [I] know that God causes everything to work together for the good of those who love God" (Rom. 8:28).

Vanilla alone is bitter; but properly mixed, it is delightful. Trouble alone is bitter; but properly mixed by the omnipotent God Who loves you and Whom you love, it is absolutely delightful!

95

"You've Got to Make Them Respect Me!"

A supervisor burst into my husband's office one morning, almost hysterical. "You've got to make those girls respect me!" she cried. "They don't have any respect for me!"

Walt was the CEO of my father's publishing house. Mrs. Clark[29] was the supervisor of the subscription department. The department seemed to have functioned well under her direction for several years, so he was surprised at her outburst.

"Sit down, Mrs. Clark, and tell me what's wrong."

"The girls in my department disrespect me."

"I respect you," he answered, "and you've certainly earned the respect of other department heads. Why do you think your employees don't respect you? Have they disobeyed your instructions? If so, follow company policy and write it up."

The company had a simple, fair, and honorable protocol for assessing an employee's apparent failure.

"No, no, nothing I can put on paper. I'm not complaining about their work."

"Then why do you feel they disrespect you?"

"Just by the look in their eyes. As manager, it's your responsibility to fix it."

Walt firmly believed that every human being deserves respect simply because we were all created in the image of God Himself. Everyone has certain rights, regardless of their age, skin color, culture, intelligence, or financial situation. But above that, Walt also knew he could not command

---

29   Name changed to protect privacy.

employees to respect Mrs. Clark. Respect must be earned, not demanded. A person in authority—parent, employer, elected official, or spiritual leader—cannot depend on his job description to demand respect. It must be earned. So Walt compassionately suggested several things that would help Mrs. Clark regain the respect of her staff—obvious things like keep your word. Walk the talk. Listen. Honor and respect them. Keep in mind the ultimate purpose and value of the job. Care about them and work for their welfare.

There's a beautiful expression of this in Psalm 15. King David asked the Lord, "Who may worship in your sanctuary, LORD? Who may enter your presence on your holy hill?" God answered him:

> Those who lead blameless lives and do what is right, speaking the truth from sincere hearts. Those who refuse to gossip or harm their neighbors or speak evil of their friends. Those who despise flagrant sinners, and honor the faithful followers of the Lord, and keep their promises even when it hurts. Those who lend money without charging interest, and who cannot be bribed to lie about the innocent. Such people will stand firm forever.

The Psalm ends with this wonderful promise: "Such people will stand firm forever." And, we could add, they will have earned the respect of those whose judgment they value.

There's a happy outcome to this tale of long-ago events: Mrs. Clark did earn the respect of her employees, and they together did some great work for the cause of Christ. That's what happens when people honor God and each other. That's what the people in my life need to see in me and, perhaps, in you.

96
Expectations and What to Do with Them

When I was a teenager, I had great expectations of what my life would be like. I don't remember hoping for fancy clothes or lots of money. But I did expect to have a husband who would love me and meet every longing of my romantic heart. Oh, yes, I also expected a house full of children who would adore me and grow up to be wonderful adults.

After I found that man and promised to love him "as long as we both shall live," I still had expectations of him. He was supposed to know, without my telling him (as if he were a mind-reader), why I was pouting. And my children, bless their hearts, were supposed to say, "Yes, Mother, you're right; thank you for reminding me," when I corrected them. Instead, they occasionally rolled their eyes and muttered, "Yes, ma'am," resignedly.

But Ann Voskamp, in her book, *One Thousand Gifts*, says, "Expectations destroy relationships."[30]

My expectations were absolutely unrealistic—not just about how happy my family should make me but, I discovered sadly, that often I expected them to disappoint me; and that hurts a relationship just as much.

Case in point, my husband Walt had a pastor's heart. He loved teaching God's Word. But he also cared deeply about the people he was shepherding and for the stranger as well. When he saw a woman alone trying to change a flat tire, he fixed it, even if he was in his Sunday best. He sometimes gave a hitchhiker a ride, just to talk to him about Jesus.

---

30   Ann Voskamp, *One Thousand Gifts* (Nashville: Thomas Nelson, 2001).

198 FULLNESS OF JOY

Once, I remember, Walt was trying to help an alcoholic keep his vow to stay sober. He kept the man right beside him for three days, whether he was outlining a sermon, visiting in the home of a new member, or meeting with the deacons. And it worked. That dear man did find a blessed release from his terrible thirst.

So I shouldn't have been surprised the one day Walt came home with a big splotch of motor oil on his white dress shirt. I don't remember how he got it; I just remember trying to get it out. I soaked it. I sprayed it. I scrubbed it. I bleached it. I hung it out in the sun. At last, it was almost gone. You could hardly see it. I starched it, ironed it, and hung it in his closet.

The next morning, Walt took out that shirt to wear. He took it off the hanger, sat down on the bed, and examined it carefully. I watched him. *If he says one word about that stain,* I thought to myself with teeth clenched, *I am really going to let him have it.*

But he said, "Libby, I'm so sorry you had to work so hard to get that stain out. It looks just fine. Thank you, dear. I'll be more careful next time."

Oops! My expectations! They can destroy relationships. Set too high or too low, either way, they hurt the people we say we love.

King David tells us in Psalm 62:1-6 how he had to learn this truth:

> I wait quietly before God, for my victory comes from him. He alone is my rock and my salvation, my fortress where I will never be shaken. So many enemies against one man—all of them trying to kill me. To them I'm just a broken-down wall or a tottering fence. They plan to topple me from my high position. They delight in telling lies about me. They praise me to my face but curse me in their hearts. Let all that I am wait quietly before God, for my hope is in him. He alone is my rock and my salvation, my fortress where I will not be shaken.

May this be true for me, that my expectations will be only from God, my Heavenly Father, who has planned His very best for me.

97
More Important Than the Checklist

I have a dear friend, a high school boy, who is interested in flying. So I invited his family and another family to dinner. The husband in that family is a seasoned professional pilot and earnest Christian, and I thought he could encourage my young friend in his quest.

The pilot spoke to the boy for a while on the importance of the flight checklist. It requires a walk-around inspection of the outside of the plane and, in the cockpit, a weights-and-balance check, the weather forecast, the radio frequencies, and a checklist for that specific model of airplane, arrival plates for the intended arrival airport, all before you call "clear prop" and start the engine. Following the checklist is an essential for any pilot, no matter how experienced.

I remember my flying instructor emphasizing the importance of that checklist. "If you skip it or neglect any part of it, you may crash and burn; and that will ruin your whole day." *Believe me*, I said to myself, *I'm gonna use that checklist!*

Then Randy asked the question, "But there's something much more important in safe flying than the checklist. What do you think it is?"

I blurted out, "Know where you're going?"

"Well, yes, that's important. But there's something more important even than that. If you are going to be a good pilot, you must have integrity . . . no matter how difficult, how humiliating, how great the pressures, you must always, always do the right thing. I remembered a conversation many, many years ago, with an airline pilot who flew a Boeing 747 on international flights for a major airline. He was deeply troubled about his relationship with the Lord because in his flight log years before, he'd falsified some hours of flight time as pilot-in-command. Because the airline had stringent testing and training requirements in place, passengers were not endangered. And he really was an excellent pilot. But his conscience tormented him. He had lost his integrity, and he didn't know how to make it right."

So integrity is essential if you are going to fly a plane. But integrity is essential in every other human relationship.

In marriage? Marriage vows are a covenant, a solemn vow spoken in the presence of God. "I will love you and cherish you and protect you as long as we both shall live."

In medicine? Many doctors take the Hippocratic Oath "to do good and do no harm."

In politics? Every president of the United States makes this promise: "I do solemnly swear that I will preserve, protect, and defend the Constitution of the United States."

The lack of integrity in business deals, in friendships, and, alas, sometimes even among some Christians is a major cause of heartache and loss. A woman who drives impaired by liquor has lost her integrity. Two teenagers engaging in sexual activity with no thought of the possible consequence of the creation of a baby, an eternal soul, have lost their integrity. An employee who flagrantly ignores his job description to further his own ambitions has lost his integrity (and probably his job!)

King David said, "I will be careful to live a blameless life—when will you come to help me? I will lead a life of integrity in my own home."

May God help us to live lives of integrity, no matter the pressures, the inconveniences, the loss of money, the circumstances, or even the disapproval of friends. God, help me lead a life of integrity.

98
A Promise I Made to My Child

She was six weeks old, this tiny scrap of humanity Walt and I had adopted. She had thrived in the five weeks she'd been in our home. But that morning, her eyes were red and swollen. She would try to open them, blink, and close them again. My first thought (because a mother's imagination tends to leap to the most sinister diagnosis) was that Judy was going blind.

When we adopted our first child, the judge had asked us, "Do you understand that if there should be natural-born issue of this union, this child must inherit equally with them?"

"Yes, of course," we eagerly answered. "That is exactly what we want. This child is our 'bairn,' our 'borne one.' We pledge her our love and care until the day we die."

I think most parents feel that way when they hold their newborn child, whether adopted or born of their own bodies. They, too, whisper, "I am committed to your welfare, little one, no matter what the future holds. You belong to me, and I will love you with all my heart and protect you with all my strength as long as I live. There is nothing you can do that will keep me from loving you. I make this solemn vow before God." And that's what I whispered to my infant daughter that morning. "If you are blind for the rest of your life, I will take care of you."

But Dr. Breme, our pediatrician, smiled at my fears. "Her tear ducts are just now developing. It's a normal condition. Use this prescription until it clears up."

Judy's eyes healed almost immediately. But my vow to her did not expire. She was still my beloved daughter, and I had made her promises I intended to keep.

Has there ever been a time, in the years since, that I regretted that vow? No, never. Sure, there have been some tense moments in our relationship. You, as a parent, understand that. Her teen years were as stressful as they are for most teens. As an adult, she has faced challenges. But never have I been tempted to break my solemn vow to her—never.

A businessman of my acquaintance signed a huge contract for a certain piece of property. A few days later, he learned that the property he had originally wanted was again on the market. So he said to his lawyer, "Look for loopholes in our contract so we can get out of it."

"That's going to be difficult, sir. We wrote that contract, so it couldn't be broken."

"I know; I know. But you're the lawyer. Find some way to break it."

In Psalm 15:1, King David asks the question, "Who may worship in your sanctuary, LORD? Who may enter your presence on your holy hill?" The Psalm enumerates several godly traits God wants to see His children develop. Verse four says, "Those who . . . keep their promises even when it hurts." That means, "I will stand by the contract I signed. I may lose money by it; it may cause me loss. But I will keep my promise."

Human relationships require trust. And we ought not to break a trust, even an unwritten one, in our relationships with others, whether marriage, parenthood, employment, or citizenship.

99
What Would You Like Me to Do?

My mother knew her Bible so well that her instructions to us children were often simply words from the Bible.

I would say, "Mother, Susie and I are having such a good time. Can I stay here for another hour?"

Mother might reply, "'Don't visit your neighbors too often, or you will wear out your welcome'" (Prov. 25:17).

Or if I said, "Mother, Grace is being mean to me!"

Mother might gently say, "'Be kind to each other, tenderhearted, forgiving one another, just as God through Christ has forgiven you'" (Eph. 4:32).

Mother's admonitions usually worked because, after all, who wants to argue with God?

Recently, I saw a waitress put into action one of the Scriptures Mother often used. (In our home, there were six girls; and most of us, I fear, were alpha females, so she needed it often!) Mother would have enjoyed watching how the waitress' reaction played out.

Walt and I were guests of friends in a posh restaurant. They'd both ordered shrimp and grits. This was a *very* Southern restaurant! But when their order came, the food was so spicy, they couldn't enjoy it. They were trying not to grumble about it, but they were very disappointed.

Our waitress noticed their discomfort. "Is there something wrong?"

"This is so spicy, we're having trouble eating it."

Of course, it wasn't the waitress' fault; and perhaps, most people ordering that dish would have known it would be spicy. But she didn't get defensive. She didn't wilt. She simply said quietly, "What would you like for me to do?"

Mother would have quoted Proverbs 15:1: "A gentle answer deflects anger, but harsh words make tempers flare."

The quiet words of the waitress helped our friends to decide quickly what they really wanted. They could order a different dish, without extra charge; but that would take time, and we were on a tight schedule. Their alternative was to decide they could endure spicy shrimp and grits. And that is what they did.

I have a friend who is always having confrontational bouts with the people who serve her. She is rather proud of the fact that she can put the "hired help" in their place to get what she wants. Do you suppose a "gentle answer" on her part might help her to get better service?

It's a Scripture that works well in every-day situations. If you're dealing with a co-worker unhappy about an assignment, "a gentle answer deflects anger." A friend dealing with a grieved friend, a father talking to a teenage son, a teacher teaching an unruly pupil, a supervisor dealing with a difficult employee—"a gentle answer deflects anger."

"As a face is reflected in water, so the heart reflects the real person," says Proverbs 27:19. Like a mirror reflects an angry expression or a kindly one, so your tone of voice will (hopefully!) be reflected in the voice of the one who answers you. It's worth a try. Remember, Mother was only quoting what God Himself said.

100
Why Not Now?

When I was a child, and Mother was making biscuits, I would read again the line that was printed on every bag of General Mills Gold Medal Flour. It intrigued me so. It was only three words: "Why not now?"

I was deeply troubled by those words. What did they intend for me to do? And why now? And why not? I finally realized they were saying Gold Medal Flour is so wonderful that someday, I would choose to use it instead of the inferior flour I was stuck with now.

General Mills started using that slogan in their advertising in 1907. It was still there when I was cooking for my own children in the '50's, and it still intrigues me. "Why not now?" The question implies that a decision needs to be made. It suggests that eventually, we will see the wisdom of making that decision. It exhorts that we ought not to waste any more time hesitating.

First Kings 18 tells the story of a confrontation the prophet Elijah had with the 450 prophets of Baal. (Baal was the title of the god the Canaanites had created for themselves. He was, like his creators, foul and disgusting. His worshipers burned their babies in the fire to gain his approval.) So Elijah set out to prove to them who was really the infinite holy God. The whole countryside came to watch. So Elijah said to them, "'How much longer will you waver, hobbling between two opinions? If the Lord is God, follow him! But if Baal is God, then follow him!'" (1 Kings 18:21).

The people didn't answer him. They needed proof. So God, in a remarkable display of His infinite power, sent fire from Heaven to burn up Elijah's sacrifice. Now it was time for the people to make a choice. "Why not now?"

It may be in your life you have hesitated to make a decision you know you ought to make. It may be a need to repair a broken friendship. Perhaps you've needed to break off a bad habit, a poor use of time, or sheer indolence. It may be that you've been so busy you haven't been the parent you need to be. Might there be someone you've valued as a friend but whose influence on you seems to be always for the bad, not the good? Is it time to end that relationship? Have you had a dream of doing some good thing for God but postponed it? Why not consider it again? Is this, perhaps, the day you need to turn from your own way and make a decision to trust Christ as your Savior? If so, why wait? Why not now? Eternity is at stake.

The prophet Moses said to the Israelites in his farewell message to them:

> "Now I call on heaven and earth to witness the choice you make. Oh, that you would choose life, so that you and your descendants might live! You can make this choice by loving the Lord your God, obeying him, and committing yourself firmly to him. This is the key to your life. And if you love and obey the Lord, you will live long in the land the Lord swore to give your ancestors Abraham, Isaac, and Jacob" (Deut. 30:19-21).

Bibliography

Adams, Douglas. "Thoughts on the Business of Life." *Forbes* online. Accessed July 24, 2024. https://www.forbes.com/quotes/2196.

Anderson, Jenny. "Many American Parents Have No Idea How Their Kids Are Doing in School." *Time*. August 28, 2023. https://time.com/6308834/american-parents-how-their-kids-doing-in-school.

Black, John, Niger Hashimzade, and Gareth Myles. *A Dictionary of Economics*. Oxford: Oxford University Press, 2009. https://www.oxfordreference.com/display/10.1093/acref/9780199237043.001.0001/acref-9780199237043-e-3816.

Bowen, Catherine Drinker. *The Miracle at Philadelphia: The Story of the Constitutional Convention*. Unknown, 2010.

Covey, Stephen R. *The 7 Habits of Highly Effective People*. Los Angeles: Free Press, 2004.

Frost, Robert. "Mending Wall." Poetry Foundation. Accessed May 27, 2024. https://www.poetryfoundation.org/poems/44266/mending-wall.

Gilbreth, Frank B. and Ernestine Gilbreth Carey. *Cheaper by the Dozen*. New York: Harper Perennial Modern Classics, 2019.

H., Bill. "Kittie Suffield—'Little is Much, When God is in it," *Church History Minute Notes*. October 14, 2018. https://bill8147.blogspot.com/2018/10/kittie-suffield-little-is-much-when-god.html.

Johnson, Chris and Eric Single. "SI's Top 100 College Football Players of 2018." *Sports Illustrated* online. June 18, 2018. https://www.si.com/college/2018/06/19/top-100-player-rankings-2018-full-list.

Keepfer, Scott. "Talent-laden Tigers can't 'listen to the noise,' says assistant coach Brent Venables." *The Greenville News* online. June 22, 2018. https://www.greenvilleonline.com/story/sports/college/clemson/2018/06/22/brent-venables-says-clemson-cant-afford-listen-noise/726276002/.

Keillor, Garrison. "Inside Garrison Keillor's fabled world of 'A Prairie Home Companion.'" July 26, 2014. In *PBS News Hour*. Radio. 10:37. https://www.pbs.org/newshour/show/40-years-counting-inside-garrison-keillors-fabled-world-prairie-home-companion#transcript.

Lippmann, Walter. "Walter Lippmann Quote." Libquotes.com. Accessed July 24, 2024. libquotes.com/walter-lippmann/quote/lbg5u0m.

More, Hannah. *The Works of Hannah More*. New York: Harper & Brothers, 1855. https://archive.org/details/worksofhannahmor00moe/page/n11/mode/2up.

Peddi, Nagabhushanam. "Unleashing the Power of the Pareto Principle in Entrepreneurship." Startup Savant. July 2, 2024. https://startupsavant.com/startup-basics/pareto-principle-in-entrepreneurship#:~:text=Software%20giant%20Microsoft%20once%20discovered%20through%20its%20research,top%20issues%2C%20maximizing%20user%20satisfaction%20with%20fewer%20fixes.

Piper, Watty. *The Little Engine That Could*. New York City: Grosset and Dunlap, 2001.

Stanhope, Philip Dormer, Earl of Chesterfield. *Letters to His Son, Complete On the Fine Art of Becoming a Man of the World and a Gentleman*. Mainz: Gutenberg Press, 2004. https://www.gutenberg.org/ebooks/3361.

Stevenson, Robert Louis. "Robert Louis Stevenson Quotes." BrainyQuote.com. Accessed June 4, 2024. https://www.brainyquote.com/quotes/robert_louis_stevenson_101230.

Stowe, Harriet Beecher. *Life of Harriet Beecher Stowe: Compiled From Her Letters and Journals by Her Son Charles Edward Stowe*. Independently published, 2016.

"Summary of Joan Miró." The Art Story. Accessed July 25, 2024. https://www.theartstory.org/artist/miro-joan.

Tikkanen, Amy. "US Airways flight 1549." In *Britannica*. Accessed July 18, 2024. https://www.britannica.com/science/disaster.

"Verbatim: Jan. 22, 2007." *Time*. January 11, 2007. https://time.com/archive/6679616/verbatim-jan-22-2007.

Voskamp, Ann. *One Thousand Gifts*. Nashville: Thomas Nelson, 2001.

Will, George. "Can Romney turn this contest around?" *The Washington Post*. Washington, D.C. October 1, 2012. https://www.washingtonpost.com/opinions/george-will-romney-running-out-of-clock/2012/10/01/55922ea4-0bec-11e2-bb5e-492c0d30bff6_story.html.

About the Author

Elizabeth Rice Handford is the wife of Walt Handford, who pastored Southside Baptist Church of Greenville, South Carolina, for thirty-one years. She is a mother of seven, grandmother of eighteen, and great-grandmother of nineteen. Elizabeth is an honors graduate of Wheaton College, holds a private pilot's license, and is a lifelong student of the Scriptures. She has written many books and Bible studies, including her best-known work, *Me? Obey Him?* which sold over 650,000 copies. Elizabeth is a regular contributing author to *The Joyful Woman* magazine.

Ambassador International's mission is to magnify the Lord Jesus Christ and promote His Gospel through the written word.

We believe through the publication of Christian literature, Jesus Christ and His Word will be exalted, believers will be strengthened in their walk with Him, and the lost will be directed to Jesus Christ as the only way of salvation.

For more information about
AMBASSADOR INTERNATIONAL
please visit:

www.ambassador-international.com
@AmbassadorIntl
www.facebook.com/AmbassadorIntl

Thank you for reading this book!

You make it possible for us to fulfill our mission, and we are grateful for your partnership.

To help further our mission, please consider leaving us a review on your social media, favorite retailer's website, Goodreads or Bookbub, or our website, and check out some of the books on the following page!

Most of us know Who Jesus is and would admit He was a good and kind Teacher while here on earth. But He is so much more than just a good and kind Teacher—He is our Savior and God and worthy of all our worship. Through an in-depth study into the book of Hebrews, Joshua West and Gary Wilkerson take apart each verse, drawing the reader to a closer look at the Man Who lived here on earth for a short time and then became our Sacrifice to save us from our sins and live with us eternally in Heaven with Him. If you are searching for something more from God, dive into this study and drink in the jaw-dropping beauty of our Jesus.

When our passions overtake us—as they often will—compulsive and addictive behaviors can set in. In *Misguided Passions and the Lord's Prayer,* Curt Richards examines the Lord's Prayer line by line and draws out comforting and reassuring insights that can be applied to the daily lives of anyone, especially those struggling with misguided passions. Richards shines a light on the beautiful universal truths found in the Lord's Prayer.

In a world that is full of chaos and change, many people turn to the Psalms to find comfort in times of stress. In *A Harmony of Two Psalms*, Guy Robert Peel Steward takes a closer look at two of those psalms—Psalm 2 and 91—and analyzes their key truths, hoping to shine some light for the reader on what the words truly mean and how they can find comfort in the God Who sees the chaos and offers rest in the storm. Be challenged in your knowledge of God's Word and learn more about some of the verses that can soothe our weary souls.